The Return to Love Playbook

Secrets to recapturing passion, romance, and commitment with the partner you already have

Debra D. Castaldo, Ph.D.

BALBOA.PRESS
A DIVISION OF HAY HOUSE

Balboa Press books may be ordered through booksellers or by contacting:

Balboa Press
A Division of Hay House
1663 Liberty Drive
Bloomington, IN 47403
www.balboapress.com
844-682-1282

ISBN: 979-8-7652-5813-2 (sc)
ISBN: 979-8-7652-5814-9 (e)

Print information available on the last page.

Balboa Press rev. date: 01/02/2025

Dedicated to

The one

who brought me home to love

CONTENTS

ACKNOWLEDGMENTS

I am humbled by the clients who have trusted me to guide them home to love. It is with deep gratitude that I thank every couple and family who has given me the privilege to be their sacred colleague in healing broken relationships. I have learned a great deal from the couples who have persevered with me to save and improve their relationships. I am also indebted to the families I worked with as a fledgling social worker. Their suffering through neglect, abuse, violence, separation, and broken attachments compelled me to dedicate myself to helping couples have healthier relationships. Through them I came to understand the destructive power of multigenerational family patterns, and why they must be corrected so future generations can enjoy a happier future.

I also thank the master teachers on whose shoulders I stand, and whose presence in my life has been nothing short of miraculous. I honor the memory of Steve de Shazer and Insoo Kim Berg, whose expertise laid the foundation for mine. Forty years ago, not only did they shape the course of my life's work, they inspired me to live my life with trust in miracles, possibilities, solutions, and the capacity of the human spirit to heal.

A special acknowledgment goes to Terrence Real and Esther Perel whose couples' therapy models, skills, and unique expertise re-energized me when I felt stagnant. Their compassionate work has enabled me to strengthen my ability to bring couples back from the brink.

To my colleagues and friends who have patiently listened and generously shared their feedback and expertise, warm thanks, I could have never done this without you! Most importantly, to my small circle of sacred colleagues, my "kindred spirit" friends who laugh with me until we are doubled over, hold me up when I sob, and never fail me, you are loved more than you know.

Dr. Deb

PROLOGUE

I am a member of the broken hearts club. Having suffered heartbreak several times, I am painfully familiar with the despair and grief that accompanies lost love. I know first-hand the disappointment of a shattered fairytale, and the fear that love would never find me again. I've survived the pain of hoping to save a dying marriage, the confusion of deciding whether to stay or go, the sadness of choosing to divorce, the fear of returning to single life, and the frustrating search for new love. If you are in any of these states of distress, you are not alone. I have been on the same journey, and may have made some of the mistakes you may be making now.

I remember the moment thirty - three years ago when my heart first shattered. My doctor asked my ex-husband to leave the room and said, "I don't find anything physically wrong with you. It seems you have chronic anxiety. What's going on with your marriage?"

As I burst into tears, what I knew in my soul began to make sense: my marriage was slowly crushing my spirit. After years of anguish, I accepted that I did not feel loved, nor were my most basic needs for emotional connection, support, affection, and intimacy being met. In sixteen years of marriage, I felt invisible and experienced a lack of intimacy, unexplained physical illnesses, and silence that had taken an emotional toll. I was both drained and baffled about what was wrong or how to fix it. I felt I was inadequate, deficient in some essential way.

When I left my doctor's office that day, something in my gut woke up. I knew that I deserved more, and I was jolted into reviewing where my life had been and where it was going. I looked into my future and asked a hard question; if I stayed in my marriage, would I be happy. After several years of reflection and therapy, the answer was, *no*. My husband refused to commit to repair our marriage, and after several failed attempts at couples' therapy, I made the daunting and devastating decision to divorce.

My love story began with a marriage that was a mistake of immaturity. At twenty-two I wed my first boyfriend, whom I'd met at the tender age of nineteen. After two years of dating, I jumped into a marriage two months after college graduation because I thought it was what you were supposed to do. The possibility of other options or the importance of my own growth never entered my mind.

Like most people, I was attracted to the familiar from childhood, and that is where my trauma began. I married a version of the parent with whom I had the worst relationship: my father. Although my dad was a decent working man, scars from a troubled childhood, an abusive, alcoholic father, and a depressed mother left him unable to truly see me or express love for me. While there was no alcoholism or domestic violence in our home, and my dad was physically present and hard-working, our emotional connection was non-existent. Although my father related to me in humor and practical jokes, as a little girl I felt invisible. My mother was warm and nurturing, but her marriage was difficult, and her needs were not met. Dysfunctional patterns were firmly embedded as they had been in the previous generations of my family.

I'm happy to tell you that the young woman who couldn't speak up for herself and was terrified to ask for the love she deserved is long gone. I have experienced so much emotional growth I hardly recognize the former me. In my post-divorce years, I have grown into a mature, wiser version of my emotional, spiritual, and sexual self. After my divorce I enjoyed years of dating that led to several significant romances, including a fifteen -year relationship that was mostly easy, peaceful and fulfilling. Thankfully, I had the joy of falling in love again, sharing easy companionship, fulfilling intimacy, and even being love sick for the first time in my life. I will be forever grateful for this long relationship, because my partner healed the damage left by marriage. Unfortunately, after thirteen years, our partnership began to deteriorate, and once again, I had to face the very painful decision to let go of love. My second break-up was an even harder gut punch than the first one, because I was truly in love, and in most ways, we were a great match. Nonetheless, issues began to surface that I could not accept, and my boyfriend was unwilling to address. By this time, I had set new standards for myself that would not allow me to accept anything less than the great love I knew I deserved.

I have severed the legacy of my generational curses, and I am no longer repeating the dysfunctional relationship patterns of my ancestors. Furthermore, I have arrived at conscious awareness of what I want in a relationship, making better choices, and have developed the skills necessary to create healthy, fulfilling love. I have achieved this through consistent hard work supported by my own therapy as well as over thirty-five years of experience as a couples and family therapist, knowledge gained in my Ph.D. studies, and many years of training in couples and family therapy.

Professionally, I have observed love and relationships through the lens of a child protective service social worker, and as a couples and family therapist. I have seen the dark side of marriages and family dysfunction, and the harm it can do to both children and adults. I've observed lives destroyed by domestic violence, addictions, untreated mental health issues, infidelity, and financial ruin. I've also seen families trapped in decades of misery, rage, fighting, silent treatment, and abandonment.

I continue to do what I do because it's an honor and privilege to be entrusted with helping couples and families heal. Among the best rewards in my practice are receiving pictures and phone calls from couples who have returned to love: a young couple with their new baby, a retired couple enjoying their travels, or a couple renewing their vows after surviving infidelity. I trust in the belief that love can be vibrant and fulfilling for a lifetime, and couples can return home to restore love that was lost. My sacred mission continues to be to help individuals and couples heal their trauma, learn new skills, break the cycle of multigenerational dysfunction, and offer their children and future generations a brighter, happier future of loving relationships.

Throughout my journey, I have learned how precious love truly is, how difficult it can be to find, and how easily it can disappear. My work has given me the opportunity to think about the importance of true intimacy; sharing friendship, companionship, fun, and open communication. I work every day to practice the complex aspects of loving, focusing on sparkling moments, gold standards, keeping the erotic fires burning, and breaking "the bad" of family legacy. So, here I am, ready to pass on the knowledge and wisdom I have experienced from my own life, and helping hundreds of couples resolve their differences and solidify their happiness. I come to you with a deep understanding of not only love's reasured gift, but the pain of heartbreak, and the resilience it takes to go beyond just living to catapult into truly grabbing life and redesigning it. I offer you my trust in the power of love and the human capacity to bring yourself home to love well, and to stay in love for the rest of your life. As you journey into *The Return to Love Playbook*, I wish you a magnificent reunion with love! – Dr. Deb

THE RETURN TO LOVE PLAYBOOK

Your heart knows the way. Run in that direction. Close your eyes, fall in love, stay there.
- Rumi, Sufi poet

Somewhere there waiteth in this world of ours
For one lone soul, another lonely soul
Each chasing each through all the weary hours
And meeting strangely at one sudden goal;
Then blend they – like green leaves with golden flowers,
Into one beautiful and perfect whole-
And life's long night has ended, and the way
Lies open onward to eternal day.
- Sire Edwin Arnold, English poet

Your task is not to seek for love,
but merely to find all the barriers within yourself
that you have built against it.
- Rumi, Sufi poet

WORDS OF WISDOM

"Love is oxygen of the soul."

-Tony Robbins, Motivational speaker, author

"Love is in us. It is deeply embedded in the brain. Our challenge is to understand one another."

-Dr. Helen Fisher, Anthropologist

"Love isn't a state of perfect caring. It is an active noun, like "struggle". To love someone is to strive to accept that person exactly the way he or she is, right here and now."

- Fred Rogers, American television host

INTRODUCTION

Hopeless, but not Serious

Rare is the person who has not known the agonizing grief of a broken heart. Of all human experiences, lost love is one of the most devastating, because love is our emotional home which heals the aloneness of the human condition. From the moment we are born, the desire to love and be loved stirs deeply within us. At its best, love is a sanctuary that heals the despair of living's challenges and provides relief from mundane daily life. At its worst, it can be a living hell, a boring co-existence absent of care, nurture, or passion.

Coming to the realization that you are no longer in love raises wrenching feelings of grief and disappointment because a dream is dying. Losing the love of your life is a universally distressing experience that hijacks the brain as raw feelings of despair, anguish, and disillusionment overwhelm. If you are in that distraught place, stuck in confusion and worried about what comes next, you are not alone, it may seem as if there is no hope to return to love with the partner you already have. You may feel like giving up because you believe it's not possible for love to last. But while worries and fears at a time like this are human, they are not truths; they are simply myths that have become popular over time.

Beliefs about long term love have their origin in the ancient English proverb: "Familiarity breeds contempt." It suggests that your soulmate will inevitably become your worst nightmare: everything you never wanted. This suggests that being exposed to anyone for a long period of time guarantees they will eventually become irritating and the very habits and qualities you originally found endearing and lovable will transform into the faults you despise. If you buy into this storyline, the assumption follows that it's impossible to stay in love with one person for a lifetime.

Nonsense. I don't subscribe to the belief that vibrant, fulfilling love cannot last. Although loving one person for a lifetime is certainly no small challenge, I believe it's not only possible, it is much easier than what you are currently doing. You may feel hopeless right now, but you don't have to throw away love. Break-up and divorce are not the only answers. There are infinite possibilities to create new aspects of love in your present and future. If you were happy once and had a good foundation, the memory of those experiences are within you and are accessible. If you had at least some aspects of a foundation of friendship, companionship, fun, open communication, ability to negotiate differences, and a vibrant sex life, you can return to love by bringing those experiences from the past into your present and future. You can create fulfilling love and a good foundation even if you never had it. You are the master of what you create, and change can happen in an instant!

There are, of course, exceptions to the rule. A relationship needs to serve both partners and the highest good to elevate both lives and prevent suffering. Couples who are crushing each other's souls and harm one another probably were never a good match. There are certainly cases of emotional, spiritual, and physical neglect and abuse that should be completely unacceptable. If a relationship is causing you serious harm, you may not belong together.

The purpose of this book is to help you return to love with the partner you already have. I believe there is hope for every couple who wants to do so, no matter how long they have been miserable. My goal is to lend you hope and encouragement by teaching you the skills that will enable you to love well and stay in love for a lifetime. I begin with a request; suspend your negative beliefs and have faith that within these pages I am sharing the best of my knowledge and skills to get you home to love. I invite you to come along with me into the field of all possibilities, solutions, and miracles.

Sparkling Point

Your situation may seem hopeless, but it is not serious. Not only is it possible to return to love with the partner you already have, you can create a magnificent love that lasts a lifetime. You already know what to do, and it is much easier than you think!

Is it worth it to try to return to love?

If you have had past heartbreaks, you may be evaluating if it is worth it to try to love again. Should you give up to avoid more pain? You can choose to isolate yourself to avoid further hurt, but that choice will not serve you. In fact, it can cause serious harm to both your physical and emotional well -being. Staying open to loving is critical because the need for intimacy and a secure bond to another has long been known to be the universal hallmark of psychological, emotional, and physical wellbeing. Our very survival depends upon it. Love is the most critical of all human needs, and trumps physical needs for food, shelter, and clothing.

Sparkling Point

It is important to stay open to loving, because the warmth of love brings us back to our emotional home. Love is the place the heart seeks from the day you are born. It

lives in every part of your soul, inside your laughter and tears. It is the essence of life itself.

Even though you may feel defeated and deflated, consider why you should try to return to love. First, whether you go or stay, you may suffer now and later if you don't consider how long you have been suffering in unhappiness. Is it months, years, or even decades? Staying trapped in a destructive, loveless relationship will take its toll on your physical and emotional health. If you are experiencing illness, depression, anxiety, panic attacks, emptiness, loneliness, or even total mental and physical breakdown, you may already be paying the price of staying passive.

Sparkling Point

Denial does not fix an empty heart or fill an empty home with happiness. The longer you linger in an unsatisfying relationship, the worse your physical health and emotional well - being is likely to become.

Second, if you don't repair what's wrong, you may repeat the same problems you are experiencing in future relationships. Couples that I see post - divorce and in later marriages often say, "I can't believe the same thing is happening over and over. I keep finding the same person with the same problems. Only the face and body are different. If I knew this was going to keep happening, I would have just stayed with my ex. Why did I even bother to get divorced, when I am experiencing the same problems I had to begin with?" I guarantee the same relationship patterns will keep resurfacing with different partners until you finally face your issues.

Sparkling Point

Relationship patterns passed down through generations tend to repeat unless you face them. How your parents related to each other was imprinted in your brain and became the template for your adult love relationships.

Thirdly, you are the blueprint for your children's future and the generations that will come after them. If you stay in denial about the state of your relationship, you are guaranteeing your kids similar misery. It's a mistake to think that if you fill your children's lives with activities, material things, and life's advantages, that will compensate for the stress of living with parents who barely speak to one another or argue most of the time. Even young children are aware their parents' relationship. They know when the "not -so-secret" secret is their parents' miserable marriage. If you expect your kids to pretend your unhappy relationship doesn't exist, their upset will most likely surface one way or another. When there is stress in a marriage, children often develop symptoms such as tantrums, school failure, social problems, or physical symptoms like stomach pains, headaches, anxiety, or panic attacks.

How many times have you heard someone say: "We're staying together for the kids?" Children can be emotionally harmed while living in a hostile marriage. Divorce research reports that children who grow up with parents in unhappy or high conflict marriages suffer as much, if not more, emotional damage than children who grow up with divorced parents. Consider the following questions: What love blueprint are you leaving for your kids' future? Will their legacy be filled with loving kindness, warmth, respect, and closeness, or distance, disconnection, and conflict? Don't they deserve better?

Sparkling Point

Your most important job as a parent is to teach your kids how to love. Excelling in sports and academics may fade away. What remains are the lessons you have taught children about how to love.

Why does love die?

Given how critical love is to human survival and well-being, one would think couples would take heroic efforts to protect their love. Why is it that life's most precious gift can easily deteriorate into a hell of disconnection, numbness, disdain, hatred, and even rage?

It is my belief that in most cases nothing is seriously wrong. Rather, couples stop putting positive energy in and get stuck in destructive patterns of interactions. Here are the six reasons why relationships deteriorate:

Stuck Point: # 1

You are stuck in the misconception that falling in love and its delightful sensations should last forever, no effort needed.

Falling in love and loving for a lifetime are two very different concepts. It is a false assumption that there is only one aspect to love: the "in love" stage. It is also a mistake to think that the feelings of being in love will last forever with no effort. One of the most common statements I hear from couples is, "We're here because we've been together many years, we're not in love anymore, and we're considering divorcing."

What they fail to realize is that love is like a newborn baby. You are handed a living thing that changes as it grows. Like all living things, it requires consistent attention, nurturing, and feeding to keep it alive. It is a mistake to assume love comes with a lifetime warranty, no care required. Taking consistent action to offer respect, consideration, friendship, companionship, listening, emotional support, affection, and sexual intimacy is required for a solid foundation that will stand the test of time. Your job as a loving partner is never done. You must remain a vigilant caretaker if your love is to survive and grow into mature adult love. Staying in love is a lifelong, evolving journey, not one moment in time. It's a call to action for you to create and celebrate its magnificence.

Sparkling Point

Love is a lifetime journey that is a call to action, not a singular event at one moment in time. It requires relentless commitment, a "never give up" attitude, and mature adult skills to sustain love for the long haul.

Stuck Point: #2

Failing to adapt to change throughout life will jeopardize your ability to keep love alive.

Change is inevitable in life, and loving relationships are no exception. The journey of life changes us all. Given the tremendous amount of growth most people experience, it is guaranteed that your partner will also change, not only physically, emotionally, and spiritually, but with respect to goals, dreams, and desires. As you both transform, the ability to continuously embrace and adapt is a key to keeping love vibrant. This requires consistent trust, commitment, and open communication. Your partner's needs should be your needs and vice versa. What is important to them should be a priority to you. Failing to adapt to changing needs will not serve you or keep your relationship healthy.

Sparkling Point

The day you make a commitment should be the beginning, not the end, of treating each other with the utmost respect and cherishing.

Stuck Point: # 3

Failing to keep standards high

In addition to adapting to change, it is crucial to maintain the high standards that you established when you got together. If those standards drop, love begins to die. Consider the standards you keep in other areas of your life. Do you stay respectful, control anger, listen to others' hurts, refrain from yelling, name calling, berating, attacking, silent treatment, and self-centeredness? Failing to stay committed to relationship "gold standards" in your love life allows coldness, hatred, and rage to fester.

Sparkling Point

Failing to keep high standards after entering the stage of committed love is a death knell for vibrant, passionate long - term love.

Stuck Point: #4

You have not learned the effective skills that are necessary for a successful long-term adult relationship.

When considering why high standards are often dropped by couples, two factors come into play. The first is that in western culture, we are neurologically wired to focus on the negative, which keeps many couples stuck in a cycle of problem - saturated talk and problem - focused interactions. As a result, little energy is focused on what I call the "sparkling moments" of joy that create fulfilling love. Partners often fail to build solutions and create new patterns of communication. Unfortunately, many people were not raised in households where healthy relationship skills existed. If you grew up seeing hostility, considerable conflict, screaming, hitting, silent treatment, disrespect, or lack of affection, you are undoubtedly carrying that trauma with you in adulthood. Coping skills from your childhood become your emotional "blueprint baggage". Sadly those behaviors tend to be impulsive and reactive and so are not effective in adulthood.

Sparkling Point

Keeping a relationship vibrant and thriving for the long term requires skills to search for the "sparkle" that is joyful and fulfilling. It also requires skills for going for the "gold" standards that are consistently maintained.

Stuck Point: # 5

You have let the flames of intimacy burn out

When was the last time you had sex, and how was it for you? I like to raise that question very early in couples' therapy because it sends the message that sex is one of the pillars of a healthy partnership. Yes, we are also going to open up that conversation in *The Return to Love Playbook*, because sex is not a sidebar topic. In fact, it is critical to your health and well-being of you and your partnership. The benefits of sexual pleasure have been well documented, and the impact on physical and emotional health is substantial. Research has also proven that the absence of sex can cause despair, anxiety, emptiness, loneliness, physical illness, and even an actual broken heart. And that's not all. Lack of sexual intimacy can cause feelings of numbness, deadness, anger, and rage.

I see many couples who have drifted into a sex - starved relationship because they have bought into the negative myth that sex doesn't matter after a certain age. They rationalize their behavior with excuses such as: we're too tired and too busy, the kids come first, it's just not interesting anymore, there's no attraction or desire left, and it really doesn't matter. The question remains, does affection and sex matter? Yes, it matters. because sex is more than physical acts. I view sex as a merging of souls, a sacred gift. When it is magnificent, it should be a celebration that feeds the essence of the self. The erotic, the joy of loving and living, is our birthright. The private bubble of intimacy not only provides pleasure, it is a source of rejuvenation and relief from the pressures of the outside world. At its best, there is presence, connection, authenticity, transparency, empathy, vulnerability, and of course, fun!

Even more important are the messages that a fulfilling intimate life gives to partners. Keeping pleasure, desire, wanting, and longing alive relays that the message that your connection is important, I'm still attracted to you, I still want and long for you, and still choose you." These messages and consistent action convey a deeper message that your attachment to one another is important. It builds components of an emotional connection: trust, admiration, friendship, and open communication.

Sparkling Point

Sustaining a passionate sex life keeps love alive and offers your partner important emotional validation. The message is that you are still choosing and desiring each other. That validation creates high self-esteem and an unbreakable bond.

Stuck Point: #6

You are mired in multigenerational curses because dysfunctional patterns have been passed down through the generations of your family.

If you have already tried to improve your relationship by yourselves or with the help of a therapist, and there has been little to no change, you are most likely stuck in dysfunctional patterns you experienced in childhood. This legacy is passed down from generation to generation and becomes deeply entrenched in your unconscious. When an interaction happens in your current relationship that resembles a childhood experience, you may get triggered into reacting impulsively with a childhood coping style.

Most partners have one or two triggers; behaviors that cause a state of intense upset and irrational behavior. When partners are triggered at the same time, emotional harm may be caused by both acting out in destructive ways. The task is to discover your multigenerational curses, how they originated, and where they show up in the present. The good news is that these patterns can be changed by managing and diminishing ineffective childhood reactions, learning new, mature skills, and destructive triggers.

Sparkling Point

Breaking generational curses requires you to examine the patterns of your family, become aware of the dysfunction that occurs in your present behavior, and committing to changing yourself, and letting your partner change you.

Given these six "stuck points," is it truly possible to return to love with the partner you already have? My firm belief is that every couple can make this change if they are committed to do so and follow through with action. This is why I have written this book, which is based on my decades of experience seeing couples give up on relationships prematurely. Yes, it does take consistent effort and commitment to return to a state of being "in love." But if you had many of the spectacular aspects in the beginning, there is no reason why you can't recreate them, love well, and stay in love for a lifetime.

Sparkling Point

It may seem impossible, but in the field of infinite possibilities, in the spirit of faith, trust, and love, unexpected miracles, surprises, new versions of the self, and a rebirth of a loving partnership can be created.

How can you return to love?

The Return to Love Playbook is intended to provide the roadmap and skills you need to restore romance and passion with your partner. The book addresses the six stuck points that contribute to couples falling out of love and being unable to find their way back. The focus is not be on what's wrong, details of problems, negative thoughts, or a complex history of your family dysfunction. Rather, the focus is on the wealth of knowledge you have about what is already going well in the present, past successes, and sparkling solutions you can imagine for your future. I ask you to make a quantum shift away from problems into the inspiring field of infinite possibilities, solutions, and miracles! I ask you to go beyond hope to trust yourself as your own best expert to return to love.

The book also includes "plays" at the end of each chapter that are intended for you to practice the changes and skills suggested and open conversation between you and your partner about "takeaways". After each play there is a page to make notes about points that resonate most for you. The end of each chapter also includes a summary of "sparkling points."

Your journey begins with guiding principles to shift your focus away from problems towards new skills and solution building. These principles provide a foundation for the work you will be doing throughout the rest of the book. Here is the list of solution focused principles that form the foundation of the book:

Guiding Principles of *The Return to Love Playbook*

Your problems may seem hopeless but they are not serious.

You are not dysfunctional, just stuck.

You don't have to know how your problems got that way.

No matter how long you've suffered, solutions and miracles are inevitable.

Your relationship can change and permanently.

There are infinite possibilities for changing your relationship.

Change will occur, even if you do nothing.

One small change can solve big problems.

If it broke, don't fix it.

You don't have to change your personality, but you will have to change.

You will need to lose old habits and practice new skills.

There's no right or wrong, only what works for you.

You already know what to do, you are just failing to remember that knowledge.

You are the best experts to design how you will return to love.

Let faith, trust, and love lead you in the right direction.

The Invitation

If you are tempted to give up and close the book at this point, take a moment to breathe. Contemplating whether or not to end a relationship is one of the most difficult decisions you may face in life. At best, it is wrought with heartbreak, confusion, grief, and disappointment. At its worst, it can trigger an emotional tsunami of hopelessness, depression, and psychological paralysis. I urge you to contemplate how much energy and motivation you have to do the work of returning to love with the partner you already have. Open your mind and heart in complete honesty with yourself.

You probably remember the hope and expectation you felt on your wedding day as you recited vows and committed for a lifetime. Articulating the words was the easy part! The real work comes when newlywed bliss fades, and you are faced with the challenge of creating love that will last. The heart and soul of long - term love and marriage involve nurturing your original feelings, hopes, and dreams through consistent daily action. It requires the building and maintaining of deep intimacy, the opening of both partners to one another on all levels: emotional, psychological, intellectual, spiritual, physical, and sexual. It also requires committing to a standard of giving, respect, and solving conflict and differences with peacemaking and repair.

The Return to Love Playbook offers you a way forward to return to those feelings of hope and expectation. It will require that you rely upon the very best expert: YOU, the most skilled observer and creator of your love relationship, well - being, wishes, desires, and longings. The work you will do requires that you use not only your rational brain, but also your heart and gut intuitions. When I begin working with a couple, I never know whether they will be successful in their attempt to return to love. I cannot predict your outcome, but I know without a doubt that hope, possibilities, infinite solutions, and miracle cures exist for every couple, no matter how long they have been miserable! I encourage you to increase your chances of success by making the following beginning commitments:

> Be bold and find courage to do and say hard things.
> Commit to change: whatever it takes.
> Be willing to look at yourself without defensiveness.
> Let your partner change you.
> Express your needs, desires, and wishes.
> Give and receive honest feedback
> Make your partner's needs *your* needs.
> Demand that you and your partner both keep high standards.
> Make sparkling moments and gold standards a priority
> Devote time to your sex life

Finally, trust your intuition and gut reaction to answer the following: At the end of the day, how will you measure your life? Will you measure your life in wealth, accumulations, and achievements? What price will you pay if those are your measures of your life? What possibilities lie ahead if you measure your life in love? You are the masters of how your love story ends. Will you choose to nurture your relationship and keep it alive? You can return to love with the partner you already have. It's so easy to love! Let's begin the journey together!

❖ PLAY # 1

Start a Gratitude Journal

This first play is intended help you view your relationship as a curious observer might. It is a way to start asking questions that can help you get unstuck from chaos and confusion.

Keep in mind that choosing a direction at this time is simply a beginning intention. It is not necessary to know your final outcome. Instead of tracking details of problems and complaints, begin with tracking appreciation. Create a gratitude journal that you can share and discuss. Enter anything your partner does for you that you appreciate – remembering to buy the milk, making your coffee just the way you like, a surprise gift of something you have been wanting. Also, create a column to track what you are giving to your partner that you hope they appreciate – wearing the outfit they love, doing a chore you both hate, doing an activity your partner loves and you do not.

Questions for discussion:

What actions are you taking that your partner especially appreciates?

Check in and ask your partner what they want more and less of?

Be specific in giving feedback to your partner using such phrases such as:

I really like and appreciate when you….

When you…that's not my favorite

Periodically review with each other those things for which you are most grateful.

Play # 1

Takeaway Notes

❖ PLAY # 2

Check Please!

In addition to consistent expression of appreciation, another play to start using right now is establishing "check in" conversations. One of the most common problems I see in relationships are the failure to communicate consistently about concerns and disappointments. As a result, hurt may escalate into anger and resentment. This can be avoided by having regular "check in" conversations where you both air issues briefly, offer solutions, and agree on next steps.

The purpose of the check - in is to work through unexpressed issues and feelings that may be festering. It's not strictly about sharing appointments and schedules, though mundane details may crop up as well. It's also a means to take the emotional temperature of your relationship. Check - ins need not be lengthy. You may wish to check in daily for five to ten minutes, twice per week, or weekly, whatever works best for you. In fact, if you are extending check - ins for hours, it means you have stopped listening, are mired in the minutia of problems, and are venting rather than solution -building. Remember the goal is not about getting 100% of what you want. Some days it may be 50/50, 60/40/ 90/10, and even 100/0! But hopefully, over time, each of you may likely get most of what you want. The goal is to reach positive agreements.

Here are a few questions to jumpstart the check - in process. Am I relaxed, managing emotions, open, not escalated, and ready to listen? Am I able to give and receive positive feedback and ready to understand my partner's needs? Am I willing to avoid blame, defensiveness, attacking, and trying to prove my point just to win an argument? Am I ready to build solutions and forgo problem-saturated talk?

Use the following communication guidelines:

Briefly express in one or two sentences:

What is bothering you?

How you feel about it?

What do you want?

Validate each other's needs:

Offer apology, if needed

Focus on giving and solution-building

Ask each other:

How are we doing?

Are you holding anything back you need to express?

Is there anything you need or want to tell me about myself and how I come across to you?

Have I communicated to you in ways that you did not appreciate?

What do you need more of from me?

What do I need to improve?

What are our goals for the week ahead?

Is there anything left unsaid at this time?

Play # 2

Takeaway Notes

INTRODUCTION

Sparkling Points Summary

It is important to stay open to loving, because the warmth of love brings you back to your emotional home. Love is the place the heart seeks from the day we are born. It lives in every part of our soul, inside the laughter we share, and the tears we weep. It is the essence of life itself.

The longer you linger in misery in an unloving relationship, the worse your physical health, and emotional well-being may become. Denial does not fix an empty heart or fill an empty home with happiness.

Relationship patterns passed down through generations will repeat unless faced and healed. The way your parents related to each other and you was imprinted in your core, and is the automatic program for your adult love relationships.

The most important job you have to do as a parent is to teach your kids how to love. Good grades, sports, and lessons fade away. What will remain are the lessons you have taught them about how to love and be loved.

Love is a lifetime journey that is a call to action, not a singular event at one moment in time. It requires relentless commitment, resilience, and mature, adult skills to sustain it for the long haul. The day you make a commitment, whether to marriage or another exclusive arrangement should be the beginning, not the end, of treating each other with utmost respect and cherishing.

Failing to keep high standards after falling in love and entering the stage of committed love is a death knell for vibrant, passionate long-term love.

Keeping a relationship vibrant and thriving for the long term requires skills to "search for the sparkle", which means the joyful and fulfilling. It also requires skills to "go for the gold, which means maintaining consistently high standards.

Breaking generational curses requires you to look into past patterns of your family, to become aware of dysfunction that is showing up in your present, to commit to changing yourself, and to let your partner change you.

CHAPTER 1

Awakening

Words of Wisdom

Your visions can only become clear when you look at your own heart. Who looks outside dreams, who looks inside awakes.

- Carl Jung, Swiss Psychiatrist

An invisible presence is trying to wake up from dream time into human consciousness.

- Dr. Stephen Gilligan, Author of The Courage to Love

Life brings exactly you what you need. We can even say that our suffering is a gift. It is exactly what you need to clean your poison, heal your wounds, to accept yourself, and get out of hell.

- Don Miguel Ruiz, Author of Mastery of Love

These days marriage ends when love ends. First, we brought love to marriage. Then we brought sex to love. Then we linked marital happiness to sexual satisfaction.

- Esther Perel, Author of Mating in Captivity

CHAPTER 1

The Awakening

All out of love

I once had a client who stated: "I'm not in love and I want out! I'm miserable and I don't have a clue what to do about it. Our love is dead and gone. Most days I don't feel anything, others days there's anger for no reason at all, and still other days I just feel sad. Now it's either constant fighting or silent treatment. We don't touch anymore: no hugs, no kisses, no affection at all for a very long time. I don't know how we ended up here. We were so in love in the beginning and I thought this was my forever person. I'm paralyzed, can't concentrate, and I don't know if I should stay or go." If these feelings are all too familiar to you, don't be too hard on yourself. You are not alone. As the famous philosopher Freidrich Nietzsche said in *Aphorism 35*, "You are only "human, all too human." At some point in the journey of a long - term relationship, most people find themselves feeling that they have fallen completely out of love.

Realizing that a relationship may be in trouble can rattle the emotions of even the most stable person. To lose love is a trauma that can rock you to your core. It's common to experience distress as a downward spiral of depression, anxiety, and fear. You may feel your brain is being tossed about by a surge of raw emotion. The effect may show up in your body as exhaustion, mysterious physical symptoms, or non-stop illnesses. Let me reassure you that what you are experiencing is normal. The journey of committed romantic love is often tumultuous. At its best, exhilarating joy gives meaning to life. But its worst, it can be pure hell, because living in a loveless relationship hurts. You may tell yourself that your unhappiness is a phase, and "this too shall pass." Yet, fleeting moments of emptiness and distance may turn into months, years, or even decades of despair and discontent. From my own personal and professional experiences, I have experienced the gut-wrenching depth of pain and disillusionment. I bring you good news: if you were in love at one time, be hopeful! You can return to love and heal your relationship, no matter how long it has been broken, and repairing it may be much easier than you think! As hopeless as your situation may seem, there may be nothing seriously wrong. It is very likely you are just stuck.

Sparkling Point

You are not alone! Romantic love and intimate connection with another person can be a tumultuous ride. The normal course of love is a complex journey of exhilarating highs, depressing lows, and mundane moments.

The invisible presence within

Your distress excites me, because it's a sign that change is on the way. I congratulate you because your pain is the first step in becoming consciously aware that you are longing for more love, passion, and fulfillment from the partner with whom you fell in love and chose. It is also a sign that you are ready to take on the work of creating major change and growth. Despite what seems to be a lose-lose situation, this awakening is a precious gift to yourself. It comes from the sense of knowing that you deserve more and are ready to grow. Think of this awakening as a message from an invisible presence within you, a loving alarm from your unconscious that something is amiss and you are ready to face what no longer serves you. Trust that this invisible presence is your internal guide that leads you towards what you deserve and desire. It is a source of strength and capability, available to help you discover the field of all possibilities and create changes to permanently heal your relationship.

You may believe this invisible presence is God, the Holy Spirit, the Universe, your gut intuition, emotional intelligence, or the wisdom of your ancestors. Choose whichever of those fits best with your beliefs. This presence exists on many levels of consciousness, in your waking life, your dreaming life, and dimensions you may not fully understand. It is in the consciousness of your ancestors and generations yet to come. Consider the wisdom of this invisible presence to be, "your internal expert" that loves you and can turn your turmoil into positive healing and momentum.

Sparkling Point:

Within each of us is an invisible presence with the ability to fulfill our deepest dreams and desires and heal wounded relationships.

Consider the messages your internal expert may be bringing you through your emotional awakening and upheaval.

For example:

> I deserve a healthy, happy, loving relationship.
> I deserve to be fully loved.
> I deserve to have my love fully accepted and returned.
> I am no longer willing to suffer in an unhappy relationship.

I deserve to have my love fully accepted and returned.

I am no longer willing to accept being neglected, unloved, or mistreated.

I am ready to set new standards for my relationship.

Why is emotional pain and upheaval a requirement for change?

You may be asking why these positive messages are coming to you through a painful crisis. It is difficult to understand why growth often takes place along with emotional pain and challenging experiences. Contrary to popular belief, pleasure and happiness are not great motivators of change. Pain is the greatest motivator meant to be endured for a little while, not because you deserve to be punished. Pain is the only way you can be woken up to the old version of your relationship. This experience motivates you to propel yourself forward toward what you deserve in a loving relationship.

The basic instincts of pain and pleasure compete for our emotional attention. The delicate balance creates a healthy level of anxiety that is a necessary part of maintaining emotional well-being. It is the interplay of pain *verses* pleasure that provides motivation for human beings to achieve, be productive, and obtain fulfillment. When pain and pleasure are equally balanced, emotional well-being and comfort prevails and there is little motivation to make major decisions or take any action that will upset that balance. It is not until the balance shifts dramatically that there is enough distress to act.

Sparkling Point

Distress and emotional upheaval are a requirement for growth and major change.

In the early 1900s, Sigmund Freud identified two basic instincts as the driving forces of human motivation. He viewed the unconscious as a benevolent, self - protective force that suppresses painful experiences in order to function in everyday life. People have tremendous capacity to tolerate a certain amount of emotional and physical pain, but are also wired to gravitate towards pleasure. When pain becomes too great, survival instincts kick in to relieve distress. Only when emotional pain becomes intolerable do we take action to change the source of that pain. Freud also suggested that when faced with intolerable pain, humans usually go to either a fight or flight response. We fight for that which is most meaningful for survival, or flee when pain becomes too great or dangerous.

Think of a time when you finally made a major life change you contemplated for a long time. Why did you finally act and make that quantum leap of change? Did you flee or decide to fight to maintain the status quo? For example, if you have ever been unhappy in a job for a very long time, the pain verses pleasure was probably balanced, and you were comfortable enough to stay. If you had work, a boss, and a salary that were sufficiently tolerable, the position was acceptable.

But if that balance drastically changed – let's say a nasty boss arrived, your work assignment increased, or you were demoted and forced to accept a substantial pay cut. Under these conditions your motivation to leave most likely skyrockets. Many people tolerate unfulfilling jobs until the pain becomes too great that they finally decide to flee, going forward full steam ahead pursuing a major career move.

This pain verses pleasure phenomenon also comes into play in relationships. When pain and pleasure are sufficiently balanced and enough of your basic needs are met, you may stay in unhappy relationship that is somewhat uncomfortable and unfulfilling. The pain is not great enough to ignite the motivation to make a change. But when the pain verses pleasure scale tips, the status quo may no longer be tolerable and the fight verses flight syndrome is activated.

Arriving to the point of moving forward to confront a deteriorating relationship is a complex process. It is not typically a decision that is made in a singular moment, but a process that involves moving through stages of vague unhappiness, conscious awareness of misery, contemplating benefits verses risks, considering all options, gathering information, make a decision, and only then move forward with action. This process may bring you to a critical crossroads: will you stay, or is it now a necessity to move forward in a different way?

Why are you gridlocked in indecision?

Now that you are consciously awake to being out of love and realize your relationship may be in jeopardy, you are faced with a difficult dilemma. Coming to terms with staying or leaving a relationship is among one of the most difficult life decisions you may contemplate. Weighing the benefits of staying verses leaving is a profoundly personal journey. You may think you are clear about your decision, but just as often your brain may be highjacked by fear and sadness as you contemplate what it would really be like to leave and rebuild your life. It can be overwhelming to consider your financial situation, how you would manage, and whether or not you would find love again. This is an extremely personal decision and only you can search your own heart for the answer. It is not the place of family, friends, nor therapists, to tell you what decision is right for you.

Well- meaning loved ones may contribute to your confusion and paralysis by warning you in disapproving ways. I'm sure you have heard some version of the following: If you are that unhappy why don't you just leave? What is wrong with you? How could you possibly put up with the way things are? Why do you stay? I wouldn't in a million years prolong that kind of relationship. It may seem to you that there are only three painful choices: stay, do nothing, and resign yourself to unhappiness and suffering, stay and try to fix a relationship that seems dead on arrival, or end it and deal with the turmoil and consequences of breaking up.

Stuck in irrational thinking

In addition to thinking you have only three choices, another factor that may keep you trapped is irrational thinking. In times of crisis, human nature seems to be wired towards negative, unproductive thoughts and questions, rather than possibilities and solution-oriented thinking. These thoughts are not "truths", they are simply beliefs that have become habit. Over time you have etched them into your brain and allowed them to influence your life. These beliefs are often the result of guilt and shame, and take the form of four types of irrational thinking: negative narratives, the "shoulds", punishing past thoughts, and "what if" worries.

Negative narratives

Negative narratives are stories, beliefs, and self – talk focused on doom and gloom scenarios, hopelessness, and that which seems impossible, rather than solutions and possibilities. Some examples of common negative narratives are:

> I don't have any hope this can be fixed, so I've given up.
> Our problems are serious and have been going on for too many years,
> The solutions it would take to fix this are too big and impossible.
> It would take a long time to heal this, and I don't have that much time.
> I would be forced to change myself, and I don't want to do that.
> My spouse tells me he/she will never change, so why even try?
> I've been trying to change my spouse for decades, and nothing has worked.
> We would have to relive history and dig too far into the past to look at how
> problems got this way, and I'm not going there.
> Our relationship is so dysfunctional we may as well give up

The "shoulds"

The "shoulds" are narratives, beliefs, and self-talk that repeat an internalized message of shame, guilt, and failure. These messages are often transmitted early in life in your family of origin, even beginning in infancy. Childhood messages may extend into your adulthood and impact your relationship in destructive ways. The messages you received in childhood are driven into your psyche by cultural beliefs, religious teachings, socially constructed norms, and gender expectations. They become deeply embedded in your thought patterns. The core of these messages is often rooted in themes of self-denigration, perceived failure, and low self-esteem.

Men and women often hold different beliefs about commitment and connection in relationships and decisions regarding staying or going. Women tend to be the keepers of emotional connection and are given credit for the success of marriage and family. As a result, this very often translates into negative self-talk for women such as: "I was responsible for the success of our marriage, so its failure must be my fault." Or, "Why couldn't I keep him/her happy? Was I not enough? Maybe I'm not attractive anymore."

Men often suffer from a different case of "the should." They tend to ruminate on thoughts such as, "I provided everything for her and the family. I did my part, why weren't they happy? That should have been enough. What else could she have possibly wanted? I thought I provided; I didn't have a clue anything was wrong."

Here are some examples of the "should:"

> I should stay because that is what a good wife/husband is supposed to do.
> I should stay because I was raised to honor my vows and commitment.
> I should stay because it's convenient.
> I should stay because I am scared to be on my own.
> I should stay because leaving will harm the family, kids, or grandkids.
> I should stay because it's easier financially.
> I should stay because I haven't dated in years and I don't want to do that.
> I should stay because I don't want to deal with the turmoil of divorce.
> I should stay because I don't have enough energy to fix our relationship.
> I should leave because I am who I am and I'm not changing.
> I should stay because leaving would devastate everyone else.
> I should stay because I would feel ashamed to fail

Punishing past thoughts

Staying fixated on past regrets, decisions, and choices causes depression because you are amplifying what you can no longer change. Ruminating about the past and blaming your partner as "the bad one", i.e. "the one that ruined the marriage", does not serve either of you. The past is over, and focusing your mental energy on what was wrong will not help you move forward because you are drilling down on events you cannot control or change. Examining the past, which is different, is only helpful because it illustrates what you have learned and can use going forward. It is useful to focus on what worked well in the past that you can bring forward into your present and future.

Here are some examples of punishing thoughts about the past:

> I made the wrong choice in a partner, so our problems are my fault.
> I didn't know what I was looking for.
> I made a commitment too soon.
> I was supposed to know how to make the marriage happy.
> I was too young and didn't know what I was doing.
> When we married, I didn't even know who I was.
> We didn't know each other and it was a bad decision to get married so soon.

I saw troubling signs in the beginning and I ignored them.
I regret the whole thing. I knew it was wrong and I didn't follow my gut.
Everyone told me not to do it and I didn't listen.
I wasn't really happy or in love at that time, I don't know why I did it.
We had children way too young. Our relationship was already disappointing.
I was running away from another bad break up and I wasn't healed.
I was escaping from a bad family situation.
I had a fairy tale in my head, and I didn't know marriage wasn't really like that.
He/she presented well in the beginning and then completely changed.

"What if" worries

Worrying about "what ifs" means you are projecting too far ahead in time. You cannot control anything about an unlived future. This will only create anxiety and waste emotional energy. Anxiety is also often related to the fear of the unknown. What if this happens or that happens, or doesn't happen? You can waste a tremendous amount of emotional energy on thoughts about negative possibilities that will never occur.

Examples of "What If Worries":

What if I spend the rest of my life alone?
What if there is no one out there for me?
What if I get sick and there is no one to care for me?
What if I can't handle it financially?
What if I stay and it makes me sick?
What if our situation gets worse and I become more depressed or anxious?
What if my decision ruins our family and friendships?
What if I get lonely and can't handle living alone?
What if I can't figure out how to organize my life by myself?
What if I don't enjoy doing anything on my own?
What if I stay and never really experience true love or happiness?
What if everyone blames me?
What if it destroys my kids?
What if he/she marries someone else?

The importance of self-care

Confusing, irrational thoughts are your brain's way of making sense of a painful situation that has you stuck in a state of fear and confusion. What you are going through is a normal reaction to crisis, and the beginning stages of grief. It's important to be kind to yourself during this period of suffering. You may feel the need to just sit with your feelings of confusion and paralysis, and that is perfectly okay. It's important not to try to suppress feelings. Allow them to flow: cry, be sad, be angry, and let yourself just be. If you try to deny those feelings, the trauma may get stuck in your body and surface in the form of depression, anxiety, or physical illnesses.

It's often helpful to lower your expectations and focus on necessary self-care tasks. If you are accomplishing some basics such as sleeping, eating, work, and getting your kids fed and where they need to be, you are actually doing quite well considering the trauma are experiencing. If you are having trouble accomplishing those tasks, do not be too alarmed. This stage will not last forever. Some coping techniques that can be helpful include maintaining a normal exercise routine, staying busy, and enjoying the company of friends and family who support you.

Committing to change: the call for therapy

When one or both partners reach the point of intolerable pain, that is often the moment they reach out for therapy. Distress and urgency are evident, and the call to a trained professional typically ends with the question: "Is there hope and can you help us?"

Here are some typical opening complaints I have heard from couples:

"I'm not in love anymore and I want to see if there is more happiness out there for me."

"I've been unhappy for a very long time, really the whole marriage, and I haven't told anyone."

"I knew this person was the wrong choice from the very beginning. I married because I felt I was supposed to. I was getting older, starting to panic, and this person came along."

"I was so overwhelmed with infatuation and lust that we moved in together after only a few months. We got married shortly after that. That was a big mistake. We didn't really even know each other. Now that the real person has surfaced, I know I made a terrible choice."

"I've been miserable for a long time, but I didn't feel I could leave because we were raising children and I couldn't break up the family, so I stayed."

"My kids are really little and I want to get out now so they don't have to be raised in an unhappy home seeing constant fighting with two parents who can't stand the sight of each other."

"I'm running out of time, I already wasted thirty plus years, and I want to be happy, even if that means being on my own."

"We've tried everything and I don't have hope that anything will help. I have no energy left to work at marriage anymore. I feel nothing. It's dead."

"What will the kids, grandkids, other families, and friends think? They think we're the perfect couple. I don't want them to know how bad things are, and I don't want to face them. I would be too ashamed."

"I'm not happy but I have a lot of years invested and I don't want to leave my home."

I can't deal with the turmoil it's going to cause for me and everyone around me If I leave."

"It feels as if only a huge miracle could fix this and that seems completely impossible. I don't believe in miracles. I'm not even sure I believe in love anymore."

"It would take too much energy to fix this relationship, so maybe it's better that I just do nothing and decide not to decide."

"Is there more happiness and someone better out there for me. Maybe the fairy tale still really exists, and I want to take my chances to try to find it."

"I want to be the center of someone's world, and this isn't working like that for me."

None of those beginning thoughts, beliefs, or feelings are predictors that a relationship will fail. And, yes there is hope for you, as there is for every couple, no matter how long your relationship has been broken. I lend hope to you now with the utmost of sincerity and respect because I truly believe many couples can repair their relationship. I have witnessed those couples who have had the courage to use therapy to rediscover the magic of returning in love. It is a joy to guide them in their commitment to change themselves, their relationship, and their generational history.

Sparkling Point

Your current thoughts, feelings, and beliefs are not truths or predictors of failure of your relationship.

Some couples begin therapy committed to doing whatever it takes to save the relationship. Couples' therapy requires self-awareness, taking responsibility for one's part, and a willingness to learn new skills. I usually ask couples if they are here to save their relationship or to separate from one another. If they respond with expressions of love and commitment, I know I have leverage and the therapy may succeed. In other cases, significant damage has already been done and the couple has waited too long to seek therapy. I am also sometimes surprised by those couples who come with a good foundation and great potential to return to love, but are unwilling to commit to do the work. If I hear a partner say: "I don't need this, I can find someone better. I have money to live wherever I want. I'm not interested in changing myself." it is difficult to move forward with therapy.

All humans have their limit to the pain they can tolerate, and sometimes both partners are at the point of no return. If they are hell bent on raging, blaming, and attacking, I do not allow that in therapy sessions. I will dismiss partners who cannot contain themselves and seem to be determined only to punish, abuse, and fight. I explain that they are not ready for the process of couples' therapy and provide referrals for individual therapy, or offer that option with me. In these situations, I know the survival of the relationship is not likely. Others bring their partner to therapy to deliver the bad news that they are done, have seen a divorce lawyer, and are leaving. From my observation as a therapist, it is painful to see the hopeful partner completely blindsided with the news that is already too late. It is a sure sign that the couple had been disconnected for quite some time, and they may be at the point of no return. The unsuspecting partner often responds with some version of this statement:

"I didn't have any clue you were that unhappy, let alone that you already planned to leave. You never said a word to me. I knew we were hitting a rough patch, but I thought everything was okay."

In the course of my work with couples over the last thirty plus years, as well as personal experiences, I have come to understand that love is a fragile, living thing. It thrives or dies according to the way it is nurtured or neglected. There is hope for every couple no matter how long the relationship has been broken. Even if you choose to do nothing, life will keep flowing and your dilemma will naturally evolve in one direction or another. Change is inevitable.

It's never too late to begin to recreate a more loving relationship with the person you already chose. If you elect to return to love and continue with doing the work in this book, I ask you to first embrace your painful awakening as a sign that change is already on the way! Hold onto the belief that there is hope for you and your partner to create a more loving relationship. As you begin this journey, even though I will not be physically present with you, I will be with you in spirit on the written page. Imagine me as your teammate in this venture, cheering you on!

Sparkling Point

You are the architect of the change you will create. You will generate the possible solutions from your internal wisdom. This is your journey, and you are a hero for taking it!

❖ PLAY # 3

Are You Waking Up?

You may have been aware for some time that something has been amiss in your life. Perhaps you've experienced a vague, nagging feeling of unhappiness that wouldn't quit. Maybe you have rationalized that this is simply what marriage is, one damn thing after another. You may have been living a life of quiet desperation, convincing yourself that sustaining a sensation of being in love is an unattainable fairytale. But if this is the norm, why are you feeling miserable and discontented? Waking up to pain and confusion is a good thing. It signals that you deserve more love, joy, fulfillment, laughter, affection, intimacy, and peace. You deserve to return home to love.

Embracing your awakening

The "play" that follows is intended to help you embrace your awakening and follow the lead of your invisible presence. Ask yourself how you may use your pain and upheaval to propel yourself forward, ask more helpful questions, and get yourself unstuck. It is also intended to help you search your heart and contemplate your own unique answers and solutions.

Contemplate the following:

Where is emotional distress and pain showing up in my life?

Is unhappiness showing up in any other relationships, and if so, where?

Is it showing up in my body, if so where and how?

What are the emotional wounds that keep surfacing in my relationship?

Are the problems in my relationship a pattern that is familiar to me from childhood or previous relationships?

Is this a pattern I observed in my parents, grandparents, or others in my extended family?

Am I stuck in role such as: pursuer, distancer, helpless victim, demanding authoritarian, or silent sufferer?

Viewing this awakening to consciousness as an opportunity to ask yourself: what are my deepest longings and needs in my relationship at this time?

What are my desires for other areas of my life?

What do I believe my strongest abilities are to fulfill these longings and desires?

My intuition is telling me to respond to this pain by...

Play # 3

Takeaway Notes

❖ PLAY # 4

Shake It Off

Getting unstuck from negative narratives

Confusion is a wonderful thing, really! You may ask, how can this be? If you are totally stuck after reading the first few pages of this book and doing the first few plays, there is nothing wrong with you! Confusion is an important factor in contemplating important life decisions and resolving dilemmas. Confusion is your brain's way of reorganizing and sorting out the potential choices available to you. When you are in a state of confusion, you are actually the most open to new thoughts, tapping into your capabilities, and discovering new strengths. If you are still confused about whether or not it is worth it to attempt to save your relationship, this play is intended to help you move through confusion past the four types of negative thinking, and into clarity.

First outline on the left side of the page, and list any negative narratives that may be keeping you stuck in indecision. Then make a column on the right side and write down alternate thoughts that counteract the negative narratives: the negative narratives, the "should," punishing past thoughts, and the "what ifs."

Negative Narratives: Alternate Thoughts:

The "Shoulds:"   Alternate Thoughts:

Past Punishing Thoughts: Alternate Thoughts:

What If Worries: Alternate Thoughts:

Play # 4

Takeaway Notes

CHAPTER 1

Sparkling Notes Summary

Romantic, committed love can be a tumultuous ride. It is a complex journey of exhilarating highs, depressing lows, and mundane moments in between.

Emotional pain and distress are a sign that you are waking up to your longing for what you truly deserve: more love, passion, joy, and fulfillment in your relationship.

Within each of us is an invisible presence that provides the ability to fulfill your deepest dreams and desires. Distress and upheaval are a requirement for growth and major change.

Four types of irrational thinking may be keeping you stuck: negative narratives, the "should," punishing past thoughts, and "what if" worries. Your current thoughts, feelings, and beliefs are not truths or predictors that your relationship will fail.

You are the architect of the change you will create. You will generate the possible solutions from your internal wisdom. This is your journey, and you are a hero for taking it!

CHAPTER 2

Aspects of Love

Words of Wisdom

We are born to love. Romantic love is a human drive. Romance can last for many years. Love can endure, bringing a lifetime of laughter and adventure, fulfilling sex, fascinating conversations, warm experiences with children, kin, and friends, and lasting feelings of passion and union with another.

- Dr. Helen Fisher, Anthropologist

What we most deeply long for if we are completely honest, is the divine: a perfect god or goddess who will never let us down. Of course, what we get instead is a mere human, as imperfect as we are.

- Terry Real, Author of US

Any idiot can face a crisis, it's the day to day living that wears you out.

- Anton Checkov, Playwrite

There will always be magic to love. You can capture the magic, find and keep real love, and make your dreams come true.

- Dr. Helen Fisher, Anthropologist

Falling in love is just one aspect of loving. Long term, committed love is a complex journey with many phases. You can grab life, learn to love well, and stay in love forever.

- Dr. Deb Castaldo, Psychotherapist and Author of Relationship Reboot

CHAPTER 2

Aspects of Love

The long and winding road

Love changes everything, and so living a lifetime together change love. Who has not struggled through the most human of experiences, the wild ride that is romantic love? Love can come crashing into your life, or unexpectedly sit beside you, as a quiet surprise. It can turn you upside down, inside out, and toss you about from the heights of ecstasy to the depths of despair. If you have ever fallen in love, you know firsthand the craziness of it all: out of control emotional upheaval, intense erotic passion, obsessive thoughts, and inability to concentrate, eat, or sleep. Falling in love is one of the most exhilarating adventures life can gift you,

If you are feeling that thrill is gone, it is not necessarily because you are no longer in love. You may just be stuck in the mistaken belief that what you felt when you were falling in love should last forever, no effort needed. However, living challenges most of us, bringing highs, lows, and mundane moments in – between. Life changes everything: who we are as we age, who we are in a family, who we are in the outside world. Love is not simply one feeling at one moment in time. It encompasses many aspects: initial attraction, passionate lust, friendship, companionship, falling in love, deeper emotional intimacy, commitment, and finally, secure attachment.

As secure attachment grows into long term committed love, difficult phases of life will inevitably happen. You may mistake these difficult phases as "falling out of love." In reality, your feelings can ebb and flow, and it does not necessarily mean you are "out of love." After all, you are only human, and it is highly likely that you will not like your partner all the time. Some days eroticism and passion may spark up and you may crave one another like you did when you first met. Other days you may not desire to be near your partner at all, and may want to be alone. There is nothing wrong with you if you don't feel "in love" all the time. No one person will fulfill all your needs and be all things at all times. There is a good chance you are not "out of love", you are just stuck in a challenging phase of life and have stopped putting effort into keeping love vibrant and growing.

Sparkling Point

Falling in love is just one aspect of loving. Long-term, committed love is a complex journey with many phases. Healthy, mature love involves growing through the initial stages into the deeper stages of love offering complete emotional intimacy and safe, secure attachment.

The ancient Greeks identified six types of love, with each one characterized by unique feelings and experiences. A mature, long-term loving relationship encompasses the best aspects of each of these six types of love and builds upon each stage as a couple navigates the ups and downs of life together. Over time, healthy romantic partnerships use aspects of each of these phases to create mature, fulfilling intimacy that can stand the test of time. The journey of love encompasses sustaining vibrancy as some aspects grow and some fall away.

Loving through ages and stages

The six types of love and their characteristics are:

Eros – joyful, romantic, passionate, lustful, high energy

Eros is the stage of love that is first experienced upon meeting someone that wakes up the core feeling of knowing that this is your person, "the one" your beloved, your lifetime partner. It is characterized by a rush of out- of -control emotions: passion, lust, infatuation, intense energy, obsession, craving, and even addiction. This upheaval of emotions are the norm, rather than the exception to the rule. Eros is "the sensual love" based mostly in physical attraction and lust. A broad definition of "the erotic" is more than just sexuality. It encompasses any experience that brings thrill, desire, adventure, and fulfillment in life. Many researchers of love have concluded that the infatuation stage of Eros love lasts days, weeks, or months, while romantic love may endure twelve to eighteen months.

Mania – obsessive, irrational, jealous, dependent, illogical

Mania love is a more obsessive style of love which often occurs when partners have already fallen in love and have agreed upon exclusivity. This is the stage when attachment is growing, and possessiveness, jealousy, and fear of rejection may surface. As dependency on one another increases, the need for reassurance about commitment also increases. Some jealousy and possessiveness in this stage is a healthy sign of a person's capability to create emotional safety for the couple and protect oneself against the potential loss of the beloved.

Ludus – playful, uncommitted, detached, multiple partners

Ludus is the Latin word for "game". This stage involves the games of courting: flirting, pursuing, distancing, and seduction. Ludus can also involve teasing, competition, and "One upmanship", with no strings attached. It is based on desire without commitment, sometimes with multiple partners. It corresponds to the normalized stage in the modern era of dating multiple people in young adulthood before making a long-term commitment.

Storge – deep affinity, special friendship, affectionate companionship, sibling love

Storge is friendship, companionship love between two people who have a deep affinity for one another, such as that experienced by best friends. It often occurs naturally and is felt as an immediate connection of "kindred spirits". Sometimes these friendships are so close that each person considers the other "family of choice." It is a cherishing, mutual love also displayed between parents and children.

Pragma - committed love and secure attachment

Pragma is often the love style that is associated with committed love and secure attachment. This is a mature love of two people who are emotionally bonded. This love develops over time and grows into a cherishing compassionate connection.

Agape – gentle, unselfish, dutiful, giving, altruistic, spiritual

Agape love is often described as the spiritual love of God, and involves love that is not envious, proud, dishonoring, selfish, or easily angered. The attributes of Agape can also apply to the unconditional love that many couples seek in marriage as well. Full respect and cherishing are important aspects of this spiritual connection.

As life goes on, love will change from day to day, month to month, and year to year. Your romantic partnership may have started out as Eros love: passionate, lustful, playful, "love at first sight" kind of love. Or, it may have begun as Pragma: an acquaintance that over time develops into more. As the initial stages of love change, you may grow into peaceful togetherness, companionship, exclusivity, commitment, and secure attachment. You may also sustain aspects of Agape love in romantic love: an unselfish, gentle, caring spiritual connection. Aspects of each stage can exist simultaneously: including passion and intimate sexual connection, comfortable companionship, deep friendship, spirituality, and a secure emotional bond.

Sparkling Point

A mature loving relationship encompasses the best aspects of each of the six types of love, and builds upon each stage as partners navigate the ups and downs of life.

Love on the brain

Although the ancient Greeks were the first to identify the six types of love, these six stages have been discussed by many modern philosophers and attachment theorists who still refer to them today. Among them is Rutgers University anthropologist Dr. Helen Fisher, who has studied the chemical changes in the brain in all stages of love and romantic partnering: falling in love, happy love, unhappy love, long term committed love, falling out of love, and breaking up. Fisher concluded that romantic love is a universal, intense need and a basic human drive that has been deeply embedded in the brain over thousands of years. Even the intense suffering we feel when love fails is imprinted in the brain. The human cravings for romance, passion, sexual lust, attachment, and desire to find new love after lost love, all originated from the experiences of our ancestors over many generations. In effect, the exhilarating joys and the desperate lows of love have been developing in humans for thousands of years.

Sparkling Point

Romantic love, with its exhilarating joys and desperate lows, is a universal, intense need, a basic human drive that has been deeply embedded in the brain over thousands of years.

Helen Fisher's brain scanning research found that three chemicals in the brain surge and ebb in romantic love: dopamine, epinephrine, and serotonin. These chemicals are activated differently in each stage of being "in love" and "out of love," and drive human behavior. Brain chemistry changes as a couple relationship progresses through these stages. In effect, the out – of - control upheaval and intensity of emotions felt when falling in love is actually driven by intense changes in brain chemistry during that phase.

In her book, *The State of Affairs,* couples' therapist Esther Perel also suggests that biological factors and hormones influence the different aspects of love. Hormones trigger desire, desire triggers lust, and lust triggers romance. Now we connect all of those aspects to happiness in long term love and marriage.

In her groundbreaking book, *Why Him Why Her*, Dr. Fisher also discusses the powerful process of attraction and falling in love. Why we fall in love and who we choose is no simple matter. In addition to the physical characteristics of ethnicity, skin, hair, and eye color, it is a complex process rooted in biology, brain chemistry, and unconscious drives. She normalized the feelings and behaviors of each stage of love in humans, and connected these to ancient human civilizations as well as the animal kingdom. Even animals experience love at first sight, loss of appetite, courting, pursuing, distancing, jealousy, possessiveness, attachment, and grieving of lost love.

Fisher's research also sheds light on the fact that this experience of "feeling in love", rooted in the chemical surge in the brain, actually cannot be sustained long term. The feelings must calm because the human brain cannot tolerate the escalated level and intensity of surging chemicals. If this high intensity did not subside, it would be almost impossible for the brain to perform other tasks, concentrate, and function in everyday life. The way love changes is embedded in our DNA, and "being in love" must change for physical and psychological survival.

Sparkling Point

The brain in love changes over time. The love chemicals of dopamine, epinephrine, and serotonin must calm so we can function in daily life.

Why we love

The endgame of the basic instinct for love is secure attachment. It is the most critical of human needs that drive decision making about romantic relationships. According to the famous psychologist Arthur Maslow, the need for love and attachment trumps all other needs: even food, clothing, and shelter. I consider intimacy and secure attachment, one and the same, created when two people open to one another to share their authentic selves and their deepest feelings and desires. Therein lies the rub. The challenge of modern day intimacy is to create secure, safe attachment, while still sustaining some aspects of love that we now expect and find so desirable in each of the stages of love: Eros, Mania, Storge, Ludus, Pragma, and Agape.

Sparkling Point

The challenge of modern-day intimacy is to create secure, safe attachment, while still sustaining some aspects of each of the stages of love: Eros, Mania, Storge, Ludus, Pragma and Agape, that we find so desirable.

The challenge of long - term love

These days, meeting this challenge of creating fulfilling long - term, committed love is no small task. Now the expectation is that committed long - term love should always be fulfilling, and if it's not, it's time to move on to someone else. In the last half century in western culture, access to divorce has become much more available for both women and men. Along with major cultural shifts came the notion that if you are experiencing a low, unhappy phase, it means you are out of love. If you feel you are no longer in love, then why is it so hard to move on, simply make the decision and let go? Why hang on and avoid loss at all costs?

The "attachment psychologists" such as psychiatrist Dr. Margaret Mahler, and pediatrician Dr. Donald Winnicott, and others studied the impact of attachment and loss of love in both human and animal infants. The trauma of a lost attachment is so devastating that they often show signs of withering away and "failing to thrive". Babies sometimes display the devastation of loss by literally refusing to eat, and becoming unwilling to attach to any other love or mother, even when a new loving, mothering figure is available. In effect, they lose their will to live or love again. The depth of despair observed in infants provides an understanding of why loss of love is nearly impossible for humans to cope with, and why adults often avoid break ups at all cost. We stay in unhappy relationships because the threat of lost love is quite unbearable.

Even when a relationship is causing emotional and physical illness, severe anxiety, or depression, many people find themselves unable to let go. Even a negative attachment is just as powerful as a positive one. You may be negatively attached to someone that is not good for your emotional and physical health, and still you stay. And yes, this is the primary reason why it is so difficult to face the possibility of failing love. It is a wonder that we are able to break attachments at all given the powerful human need for love. An attachment bond to a partner provides emotional safety and security, and makes all seem right with the world, until it doesn't.

I challenge you to expand your idea that if you no longer feel the thrill being "in love" your relationship is doomed to fail, and the only solution is to move on and search for someone else. There is much more to loving one person for a lifetime than the romance and thrill of the stage of "being in love". The entire journey, with its many aspects, is certainly full of ups and downs and periods of uncertainty. If you choose to continue on your love journey and do the work of creating change, I guarantee that there will be great joy and great pain, because relationships are just like life: one damn thing after another!

I also bring you a message of hope. It is possible not only to return to love and stay there, it is possible to create a better love than you ever had before with the partner you already have. If you work at it AND play at it, you can sustain fulfilling love. It's going to take commitment, effort, and a willingness to self - reflect and change yourself. The task is to create lasting fulfillment and joy that returns you home to love. Your next challenge is to take a measure of your love, search your heart, and decide if this is work you want to do.

❖ **PLAY # 5**

Back to the Future

Long-term committed love is much more than "feeling in love." The romantic phase of "falling in love" is only one aspect of loving. It is an experience that will change over time as life changes you and your partner. Loving for a lifetime is a complex journey with many aspects and phases.

In this meditation/visualization practice, I invite you to allow yourself to go on a journey to imagine a future version of your relationship. If your partner is willing to do this play with you, it will add to your experience if you sit or lie next to one another comfortably and hold hands. Take whatever time you need, there is no correct amount of time, only that amount of time that you need.

If you have never meditated or visualized before, not to worry. No, you're not going to swing a watch and turn yourself into a chicken! You are simply going to go inward to a more relaxed state to access your own creativity, intuition, and sense of knowing.

Different than sleep, in meditation and self-hypnosis, deeper levels of awareness are accessed naturally in everyday life. Think about times in your day when you may be driving, watching a movie or TV show, or in deep thought, and you let yourself go to immerse fully into the experience. Those are times when you are most likely deeply relaxed and in a deeper state of consciousness.

If you have trouble relaxing or feel bothered by either racing thoughts or outside noises, simply accept those experiences, and do not judge or criticize yourself. Let it be, and let your thoughts wander or race if that is what you are inclined to do. Trust that your unconscious mind will still be able to create learning and new awareness for you in the experience. You may or may not be impacted by this play immediately, or you may remember and gain new understandings later. If you feel it is difficult to do this while you are reading it, I suggest you tape yourself reading it aloud, then play it, use it to guide yourself through the experience, and focus on relaxing, listening, and experiencing whatever comes to you.

Let's begin now.

Allow yourself to get into a relaxed position either seated or lying down on your back. It is time to center yourself and let your unconscious mind take over and contemplate ridding yourself of your negative narratives, focusing your energy towards more productive alternate thoughts. Let yourself drop down into relaxation and a deeper level of your own sense of knowing and intuition. Trust that you will know what you need to teach yourself.

Begin to pay attention to your breathing and concentrate on slowing down, breathing deeper with every breath. With each inhale imagine taking in refreshing, rejuvenating, pure, life - giving air. With each exhale imagine blowing toxins, worries, and problems away from your body.

Imagine filling your body with clear blue sky as you drain your troubles out through your feet. Drop down into your heart space and pay attention to the beating of your heart.

Now starting at the top of your head, begin to relax every muscle. As you scan down through your body, picture each muscle relaxing and loosening. Continue to focus on relaxing downward, through your head, temples, neck and shoulders. Then continue on with relaxation flowing through your shoulders, back, torso, and arms and out through to your fingertips. Continue breathing deeply as you continue to relax down through your legs and feet, down to every single toe. Continue breathing deeply and slowly. As you continue to relax, do not allow any outside sounds to disturb you.

Now whisper these phrases to yourself three times:

> "Thank you for the lessons I am about to receive."
> "Thank you for the lessons I am about to receive."
> "Thank you for the lessons I am about to receive."

Then whisper three times:

> "I invite in that which I desire."
> "I invite in that which I desire."
> "I invite in that which I desire."

Then whisper three times:

> "I trust in my own sense of knowing what is meant for me."
> "I trust in my own sense of knowing what is meant for me."
> "I trust in my own sense of knowing what is meant for me."

Now we're going to take a journey through time into the future of your relationship.

Begin by visualizing walking down a set of stairs, until you reach the bottom and the beginning of a path.

Continue walking comfortably and safely on the path until you arrive at your chosen destination, a place where you wish to be to view the future of your relationship.

Now look ahead into your future and allow yourself to see what your future relationship looks like.

What is the vision that comes to you?

Who is there and what are you and they doing?

What is the feeling you are sensing of this experience?

Stay there for as long as you like, observing your future.

When you are ready to return to your room, imagine walking back to your path towards the steps, coming back up to your present.

When you are ready, in the next few moments, come on back up your steps counting 10, 9, 8, 7, 6, 5, 4, 3, 2, 1, and arriving back to the present. Allow yourself a few moments to open your eyes and re-orient yourself to the physical space.

If you prefer to just sit with the experience and let it develop in your unconscious.

If you are open to processing your visualization, when you are fully alert and ready, take as much time as you need to answer the following.

What vision presented itself to you? Describe in as much detail as possible.

If you were with someone, describe that person. If you were with yourself describe you. Describe the feelings surrounding you, either in relationship to the other, or to yourself. Be sure to focus on the feelings, such as love, joy, comfort, peacefulness, emptiness, fear, sadness, loneliness, anger.

Referring to the six stages of love: Eros, Mania, Ludis, Storge, Pragma, and Agape, to describe what aspects of love you saw in this future vision of your romantic partnership.

What sparkling moments did you see yourself and your partner creating in this version?

What gold standards did you see yourselves upholding?

How do you feel about the love experience you saw? Were you feeling happy, fulfilled, satisfied, and vibrant? On a scale of 1 to 10, rate how much happiness you felt in this visualization. Was it happy enough for you?

Now ask: "What is this vision of my future teaching me, and what lessons am I meant to gain from it?

What clarity does this experience provide to you about your current decision making?

If you had to decide right now about your relationship, what would you choose and why?

Do not judge yourself or feel disappointed if you have difficulty discerning the lesson right away. Answers and creative ideas may come to you in many different ways and at different times: in your sleeping and dreaming hours, upon waking, or throughout your day. You may also find answers come to you through other people, song lyrics, or other experiences you observe. Learning and answers may also come to you when you least expect it in the in the days, weeks, or months ahead.

Play # 5

Takeaway Notes

❖ PLAY # 6

Re-awakening Your Sparkle

Even though your situation may seem hopeless and serious, in reality, it is not. You may think it is too difficult to re-create love, but it is actually very easy! I am firm in my commitment that there is hope for every couple, no matter how long they have been miserable. Most relationships are absolutely repairable if you are committed to putting in the work. A great way to begin your repair is to stop focusing on the details of your problems and instead intend your energy on "stacking the sparkle": the good and the fun times. The first step of healing your relationship is to start warming up to one another again, through fun, joyful experiences.

Make a "sparkling moment" date

Commit to at least two dates per week. If you are stuck in getting started, alternate taking turns to plan your dates, so that you are each initiating and the responsibility is not falling on one partner. Guidelines for dates are a must. It is critical that dates be protected time, separate from family time with kids and extended family. There also must be agreement that this is guaranteed "problem free time". Leave your problems, issues, and concerns at home! Do NOT raise them on date time! The purpose of date time is to reconnect and enjoy one another.

To create sparkling moment date ideas, it is useful to search for ideas in three areas: present, future, and past. I invite you to think first about what you are doing right now that you would like to increase. It is also extremely useful to envision a future of new sparkling moments that you create with new adventures. If you get stuck, you can also think back to how your relationship began in the first place. You most likely began with many sparkling moments: having fun, getting to know one another, going on dates, becoming friends and good companions. It is often easiest to begin by bringing the memory of those experiences forward to re-create in the present.

A date does not need to be a huge production or expense, such as a fancy dinner or weekend away. Think of the smaller, everyday things you enjoy: going for a walk, a drive, getting coffee, having a small wine and cheese party at home, movies, bowling, thrift shopping, local farmers markets, dance lessons, yoga, pickleball, tennis, golf, lectures, concerts, cooking, or reading a book together.

First choose several times that you can commit to protected date time:

Here are some questions to help you generate your sparkling moment date time ideas:

What are you already doing together now that you enjoy and would like to do more?

Brainstorm and list 10 activities that you find the most enjoyable.

Make a list of activities you currently find enjoyable to do with friends. Discuss that list with your partner.

What interests, hobbies do you share together?

What interests or hobbies do have individually?

What are you willing to do occasionally that you may not like but your partner likes?

If you are stuck with no new ideas in the present, let yourself be creative and imagine things you want to enjoy in your future, and things you always wanted to learn or do.

What can you begin to do together right now?

If you are still stuck with no new ideas, then return to your past to search for ways you had fun and were good companions when you first started out? How did you spend time together then? Did you enjoy exploring the city, or hiking in the country? How and where did you have the most fun.

Play # 6

Takeaway Notes

❖ PLAY # 7

For Play: Re-igniting the Flame

When was the last time you had sex, and how was it for each of you?

Tell me about touch in your relationship.

How often are you holding one another until completely relaxed, no expectation of sex?

How many hugs and kisses are you getting and giving each day?

How is your "for play" game?

The questions above are critical to address in order to begin to heal your relationship and return to love. I ask these questions in the beginning of couples' therapy because I consider healthy intimacy a requirement for the success of long-term, committed love. All types of touch: comforting, affectionate, and sexual, are healing to body, heart, and soul. Your partner's and your needs for intimate touch are not optional. The need for physical touch is deeply embedded in every other aspect of relationship: emotional, intellectual, and spiritual. Love is a verb, and therefore you have to DO love, MAKE love. The act of touch is among the most important ways you can SHOW love. If touch has dwindled down to nothing, it is critical to take consistent action to re-ignite the flame and start warming back up to each other.

The intention of this play is to provide you with questions and tasks to help begin to re-awaken the flame of "FOR PLAY": comforting, affectionate, and passionate touch. Let's start by re-visiting the questions from the opening above, then contemplating and answer some additional questions below:

When was the last time you had sex, and how was it for each of you?

Describe how you feel about touch in your relationship?

How often do you hold one another? Are you getting to complete relaxation and comfort when you are holding?

How many non-sexual hugs and kisses are you getting and giving each day?

How is your foreplay game?

Ask yourself if you are initiating and participating in affection and intimacy at least part of the time? If not, what is standing in your way?

What do I know about my partner's needs and desires for physical touch?

What actions can you take to provide for those needs and desires?

What are your physical needs and desires?

Are you clearly expressing those needs to your partner? If not why? How are showing love through actions of touch?

What actions make your partner feel the most desired?

What actions by your partner make you feel the most desired?

On a scale of 1 – 10, how much am I willing to commit to making touch, affection, and sexual intimacy more important than other commitments?

Tasks "for play":

Commit to minimums:

> 6 hugs a day – at least 20 seconds
> 6 kisses a day – at least 6 seconds
> 6 small compliments a day – may include touch, texts, emojis

Play # 7

Takeaway Notes

CHAPTER TWO

Sparkling Points Summary

Falling in love is just one aspect of love. Long-term, committed love is a journey with many aspects. Healthy, mature love involves growing through the initial stages into deeper emotional intimacy and safe, secure attachment.

Romantic love, with its exhilarating joys and desperate lows, is a universal, intense need and a basic human drive that has been deeply embedded in the human brain over thousands of years. The brain in love changes over time. The love chemicals of dopamine, epinephrine, and serotonin must calm so we can function in daily life.

The challenge of modern-day intimacy is to create secure, safe attachment, while also sustaining some aspects of each of the stages of love: Eros, Mania, Ludus, Pragma Storge, and Agape, that we find so desirable.

CHAPTER 3

To Stay or Go

Words of Wisdom

Two roads diverged in a wood, and I took the one less traveled by, And that has made all the difference

- Robert Frost, American poet

Your visions can become clear only when you can look at your own heart. Who looks outside dreams, who looks inside awakes.

- Carl Jung, Swiss psychiatrist

You must row your own boat to move forward.

- Katharine Hepburn, American actress

Everything that irritates us about others can lead us to an understanding of ourselves.

- Carl Jung, Swiss psychiatrist

CHAPTER 3

The Fork in the Road

Your awakening to unhappiness about the state of your relationship is only the beginning. What a beautiful gift you have just accepted for yourself! It's time to face your relationship head on: either commit to taking on the work to create better love, or move on. You deserve to pry yourself from mediocrity and have a spectacular love, one that sustains and brings fulfillment to both you and your partner Isn't that the sole purpose of loving one another?

Awakening to a conscious awareness that you are desperately unhappy brings you to a fork in the road. You now face the dilemma of a life changing decision: do you stay or do you go? It may seem you are stuck in a lose/lose situation: unable to cope with staying, and yet unable to face the idea of leaving. You may be overwhelmed by paralyzing confusion, ruminating over questions such as: "Now what do I do? How will I ever sort out which way to go? Is there any way out if I can't even imagine a first step?" In this moment of distress, it is normal to be flooded with feelings of confusion, panic, and fear.

Although such emotional disturbance is tremendously painful, it is actually a beautiful gift, a signal that you are no longer willing to tolerate misery in your love relationship. You are moving towards new standards, opening up to the possibility of a leap of change, and longing for more connection, togetherness, passion, harmony, and peace. This is a sign that your self-love and emotional health are growing.

An important step to relieve anguish and confusion is to gather facts and take a rational approach to measuring the benefits verses the negatives of your relationship. In this chapter, the focus is on assessing your foundation and beginning to identify whether you want to stay or go. It begins with analyzing which parts of your relationship are healthy, which are unsatisfactory, and which need improvement. No one, not family, friend, or professional can determine for you whether you should stay or go. Only you can do the soul searching to discover what is right for you. There is no right or wrong. This is your journey to take.

Our throwaway culture

Unfortunately, commitment does not hold the same meaning it once did. We live in a "throwaway" culture and have drifted into a collective mindset of "easily disposable" partners. Many changes over the last half century have contributed to this trend. There is easier access to divorce, multiple marriages have become common, and many people forego marriage altogether. In the age of social media and dating apps, other potential partners have become more available. Although certainly there are important positive aspects to these cultural changes, the solution to throw away a committed relationship and start over can be tempting.

A prevailing fantasy is that if you can simply find a different partner, all your problems will disappear, and a new person will bring everlasting happiness and passion. I have often seen couples give up too quickly, running off to dating apps and divorce lawyers before they make any real effort to repair their relationship. Sometimes they have let issues fester for decades, to the point of irreparable damage. Some people never have the courage to try couples' therapy or they give up after a few sessions. Many do not try separation before making major decisions, only to regret it later.

I have also had clients in second and third marriages return to me for more couples' therapy with their new partners. I often hear some version of the following. "I was so busy blaming my partner and pointing the finger at them. I thought if I just found a better partner everything would change. Now the same exact thing is happening with a different person who I thought would be a better choice. Divorce didn't cure anything. I imagined being single and dating would be fun, but it just feels like a drag and a waste of time. I should have just stayed married and worked out these issues with my ex. Now I have to do it with someone else anyway. Finding another person changed absolutely nothing."

I usually recommend that couples make a commitment to try therapy for at least three to six months. If you decide to end the relationship, your recovery will be healthier if you can walk away knowing you committed to doing everything possible to make the relationship work. There are fewer regrets for those who really take their time and don't act impulsively. Given the importance of love and attachment to overall health and well – being, isn't it worth it to contemplate your choices before you make a rash decision?

Sparkling Point

It's tempting to choose the easiest way out and flee, rather than commit to work through difficulties with the partner you already have. Separation and divorce are not a cure - all.

Finding a new partner often results in repeating the same problems you had with an original partner in the next relationship, and the next after that, if you do not take the time to examine yourself. You must look at what you bring to relationships, who you chose, and what has gone wrong. Staying in denial leaves you doomed to repeating the same dynamics over and over. Since relationship patterns are passed down from generation to generation, they are often repeated unless someone takes the time to face them, do the hard work to break destructive cycles, and create new improved patterns of relating. No matter what you eventually decide, it is important to examine the part you in your relationship and choices you made that led to its outcome.

Sparkling Point

Unless you do the work of changing inherited relationship patterns, there is a high likelihood you will repeat those patterns in every new relationship. Finding a new partner solves nothing.

The plays you are asked to practice focus on how you can begin to move out of confusion and paralysis to evaluate your desire to stay or go and assess the foundation of your love relationship. You will be measuring three aspects that are critical to your decision making. I recommend that both partners complete plays #7 and #8, since play #9 is intended for the two of you to practice together using your information from plays #7 and #8.

The three areas of assessment are:

> Your personal feelings and level of happiness/unhappiness
> The core foundation areas and health of your relationship
> Your partner's feelings, desire, and level of commitment

Deciding about the future of a relationship is a very personal process that requires you to look within your heart. The task is to discover what you really want, what needs to change, and whether you are sufficiently fulfilled to stay or go. There is no pressure to complete these plays in any amount of time. Take as much time as you need to allow yourself to contemplate the questions and answers that follow.

One key to moving forward is to free yourself from negative, unproductive self-talk and questions. The goal is to shift to thoughts and questions that help you clarify your feelings and state of well-being. This process of gathering new answers and useful information can be helpful in reducing your fear and anxiety about the unknown. In addition to completing the "plays" that follow, you may also seek the advice of friends, family, or a therapist to add to your information. I also suggest consulting a lawyer, financial advisor, and a real estate agent to help you seriously assess practical questions. Gathering facts about legal, financial, and living arrangement issues can help to relieve emotional distress.

Measuring your foundation

Step two is to assess the strength your relationship's foundation. Think about your actual physical home, which is a reflection of the self. If your home is peaceful and pleasing, or chaotic and disorganized, it reflects the energy you and your partner both bring to your foundation. Not only is the foundation important for you now, it is also the blueprint for your children's future relationships.

The four pillars

The four pillars to the foundation of a healthy relationship are: friendship and companionship, the ability to solve differences, managing anger and upset, and intimacy. These four pillars are intertwined, and each depends upon the strength of the other. Think about a table with four legs. If one leg is absent, the table would topple. In this play, you will be assessing the strength of your four pillars, present, past, and future. The purpose of looking at three time periods is to identify which pillars have been strong in the past, which are currently strong now, and which you can imagine will be strong in the future. Hopefully, the deep dive into your own heart, measuring the strength of your "bones", and the contemplation of the way forward will bring you to a place of clarity.

Taking the Deep Dive

On a scale of 1 to 10, rate your feelings about your current relationship and your decision - making process. Then you contemplate a few deeper questions that will hopefully help clarify how you want to move forward. You may find some questions will resonate for you, and others may not. The questions are designed to open up multiple opposing viewpoints.

When answering the scaling and contemplation questions, trust your intuition and go with the first number that comes to mind. Make no judgements about your answers. This is an opportunity for you to search your heart for your own unique answers. There is no right or wrong number or answer, only what your thoughts, heart, and gut intuition already know is true. Remember that you are your own best expert and guide. Trust your internal sense of knowing that have your best interests at heart.

On a scale of 1 to 10, with 1 being low and 10 being high, give yourself a number rating for each of the following:

How happy am I?

How unhappy am I?

How much do I feel loved, nurtured, and nourished in my relationship?

How much do I feel like doing loving, nurturing, and nourishing things for my partner?

How much do I feel seen, heard, and understood?

How much do I feel my partner and I have each other's back?

My partner and I are good companions and friends.

We have fun in each other's company.

I admire and have pride in my partner when in public and in social situations.

I am fulfilled by our level of physical intimacy and affection.

I am satisfied with how we communicate with each other.

We are good at solving differences and conflict.

Our life goals and dreams match up well.

How much does my relationship add to my life?

How much do I want to keep my relationship?

How much do I want to end my relationship?

How much energy do I have to work on my relationship?

Now, some questions for further contemplation. Describe specifics that come to mind:

Is my relationship more helpful or harmful to my well-being and happiness? How?

What are the benefits verses the risks of staying in my relationship?

Do I feel peaceful and happy; or distressed and unhappy most of the time?

What are my reasons for staying?

Why am I contemplating leaving?

What are my expectations about being in love verses loving for a long time?

Now that you've used the rating scale of 1 to 10, and completed your contemplation questions, return to your original rating number. What number would you assign to your relationship now? Has there been a change in your number or did it remain the same? If it changed, take some time to contemplate why, and write down your thoughts.

How do I envision my future if I stay? Can I live with this version of my life?

How do I envision my future if I go? Can I live with this version of my life?

What do I appreciate about being in this relationship?

What do I appreciate about my partner?

How do I feel about myself in this relationship?

What loving actions am I currently using to show my partner love?

What loving actions is my partner showing me?

What are your ten happiest moments so far in this relationship?

Play # 8

Takeaway Notes

❖ PLAY # 9

How Strong Are Your Bones?

For each of the four pillars listed below, describe your strengths; in the past, present, and future. Feel free to write comments under each question and use the same rating scale of 1 to 10 for each pillar. The four pillars of a healthy foundation are:

Togetherness: the glue of companionship, friendship, fun, and joy
Communication: complete opening to one another on all levels
Conflict resolution: ability to navigate and solve differences and conflict
Physical intimacy: non-sexual affection and sexual connection

The Glue of togetherness: companionship, friendship, fun, joy

Questions to contemplate and rate:	Ratings:
How much quality time do you spend together?	#_____
Do you provide friendship and support to one another?	#_____
Do we have pure joy, fun and problem-free time together?	#_____

1. **Communication of feelings, needs, and desires**

How open are to communicating a full range of authentic feelings to one another?   #_____

2. **Positive resolution of differences and conflict**

Are you able to reach positive resolution of differences quickly?   #_____

Are you able to give and receive feedback to one another without becoming insulted, argumentative, or explosive?   #_____

Are you both able to give and take to reach acceptable compromises?   #_____

3. **Physical intimacy, affection, touch, and sexual intimacy**

How satisfied are you with the amount of intimacy in your relationship?   #_____

Is your intimacy consistent on a daily basis?   #_____

Are we able to openly express our physical needs to one another?   #_____

Now that you have completed Plays # 7 and #8, take as much time as you need to contemplate how you are feeling. There is no need to pressure yourself to make a decision at this time. Allow the answers to become clear to you over time. Trust your intuition to provide you with the answers you seek. They may not come to you immediately, but you may begin to receive them in your waking life, through dreams, messages through spiritual practices such as meditating and praying. Your body may also give you signals of what the right decision is for you at this time. If you find anxiety or depression have increased, it may be a cue that you are heading in the wrong direction for you.

If you have rated yourself above 5 on many of the questions, you may interpret that to mean you have a significant desire to remain in the relationship and work towards improving it. If you rated many answers below 5, you may be leaning towards leaving. If you rate yourself a 5, you are stuck in the middle, most likely because the pain and pleasure of the relationship is equally balanced. You may not be in enough pain to act at this time. If you are at 1 or 0, you may be fairly sure you want to end the relationship.

Allow yourself to explore whether or not you have reached more clarity about which direction you wish to take.

Play # 9

Takeaway Notes

❖ PLAY # 10

The Fork in the Road

Choosing The Way Forward

Step 1: Sharing Takeaways from Plays # 7 and 8

Your next step is to share feedback with each other about your takeaways from plays #7 and #8. The next step is to come together for some courageous conversations to assess each other's interest and commitment to moving forward together or apart. It's going to take some bravery, honesty, and good listening to do this part. If, after doing so. it seems as if you are both committed to moving forward and repairing your relationship, then move on to the next part of this play. If you are leaning towards separation and closure move down.

Step 2: Create a Working Relationship of Appreciation, Compliments, and

Gratitude

Now that you have decided to move forward to repair your relationship, we are going to begin with a communication skill that will set the tone for your work together. It is a critical skill to use in your daily life and in times of conflict. If you begin conversations with compliments, gratitude, and appreciation, you will be creating an environment of emotional safety. The mind responds to safety by opening up to what is coming next and focuses on receiving a message. You can trust your partner to not harm you. By leading with compliments, gratitude, and appreciation you create infinite possibilities for courageous conversations focused on solution building, rather than escalating into hurtful lashing out and escalation into arguing and fighting.

The unconscious mind is very literal. If you begin conversations with criticisms, complaining, demeaning, or dismissing feelings, the unconscious may shut down. In effect you are telling yourself this doesn't feel good, it is not serving me or us, it is harmful, and not helpful, and I must protect myself from further harm. No one feels emotionally safe being the brunt of that kind of negative communication.

Independently contemplate and answer the following as specifically as you can. Take as much time as you need, and afterward share your statements of gratitude, compliments, and appreciation with one another.

The characteristics I admire about you the most are:

I am most appreciative of these loving actions that you do for me:

You have added to my life and made it better in these ways:

I am lucky to have you because:

Step 3: Signing on for Commitment to Each Other

Take a leap of faith and lean into the hope that you will be successful on this journey by both making the following commitments:

Our Commitment To Each Other

I am willing to:

> Make improving our relationship a priority
>
> Take responsibility for my part in the relationship
>
> Do more of what is good for us as a couple, even if I don't feel like it
>
> Share myself, my needs, and my desires openly and honestly
>
> Stay open to receive and accept feedback you give me about myself
>
> Give you what you want and need
>
> Take a little bit of action every day
>
> Promise not to give up even when it is not going well
>
> Let you influence and change me
>
> Suspend threats of ending our relationship while we are doing this work

Choosing separation or relationship closure

After sharing your feedback from Plays #7 and 8, if you are still feeling unsure and confused, or you are leaning towards separation or ending your relationship, there are more options you may consider. At this point, I recommend that you not make any big decisions before trying smaller steps, especially if you are considering ending your relationship.

Begin to experiment on your own with being comfortable out of your relationship. This may help you gain clarity, and may also signal to your partner that you are seriously unhappy. Often this is a necessary wake up call to break destructive patterns. If you are still confused, unsure or uncomfortable, you may wish to:

Do nothing and continue as you are.

Make a commitment to creating a more loving relationship.

Consider separation and taking steps towards that end.

Seek out guidance from someone you trust: friends, family, confidantes, mentors, spiritual advisors, or professional therapists.

Obtain a consultation to get accurate information about the legal and financial aspects of separation and divorce.

Speak to a financial advisor for accurate information about your financial risks and well-being.

Begin your own psychotherapy to clarify your next steps

Explore potential housing options for yourself.

Try small separations, a few hours, a day, or a weekend to yourself. Spend time in an area where you think you may like to live.

Do not communicate with your partner during these periods of separation, unless you have children.

Try an in - house separation: stop eating together, communicating, and separate money. If after your assessment in plays #7, #8, and #9, you are feeling that you are suffering too much, the risks outweigh the benefits, it is more harmful than helpful to stay, and you have no emotional energy to work on it, then the relationship may no longer be the right match for you at this time. It may be best for you to move on in a different direction.

Play # 10

Takeaway Notes

CHAPTER 3
Sparkling Points Summary

Though it's tempting to choose the easiest way out and flee, rather than commit to work through difficulties, separation and divorce are not a cure all. You will most likely observe the same problems in the next relationship, and the one that follows that. If you do not take the time to examine yourself, what you bring to relationships, whom you chose, and what has gone wrong, you are doomed to repeat the same dynamics.

PART 2

The Sparkle and Gold

CHAPTER 4

Searching for Sparkle

Words of Wisdom

We often ask, "What's wrong?" Doing so, we invite painful seeds of sorrow to come up and manifest. We feel suffering, anger, and depression, and produce more such seeds. We would be much happier if we tried to stay in touch with the healthy, joyful seeds inside of us and around us. We should learn to ask, "What's not wrong?"

-Thich Nhat Hanh Vietnamese monk and peace activist

If one advances confidently in the direction of his own dreams, and endeavors to live the life which he has imagined, he will meet with a success unexpected in common hours.

- Henry David Thoreau, Poet, Author of *Walden*

Whatever you can do or dream, begin it. Boldness has genius, power, and magic in it.

- Johann Wolfgang von Goethe, Goethe Couplets

A relationship is an art. You have to keep your half perfect. You are responsible for your garbage. If you dig around in your partner's garbage, you will end up with a broken nose.

- Miguel Ruiz, Author of Mastery of Love

CHAPTER 4

Searching for Sparkle

'Tis the season to sparkle

How do you begin to shift away from whatever is wrong and its source? In this chapter the focus is on defining relationship sparkle, how to create it, and why it's important. You will be learning the specifics of how to get back lost sparkle and create even more sparkle than you ever imagined possible. This is the beginning of you and your partner becoming your own best experts to create exactly what you want in the next chapter of your love story. It may surprise you to know you already know what to do!

Let's begin by doing a "180" away from problems and towards "relationship sparkle". What follows is a step-by-step plan for creating a sparkling relationship. It will include getting unstuck from limiting beliefs, turning trash talk into sparkling conversation, making a big shift, and easy techniques to "stack your sparkle". You may reorder the steps in this chapter if it makes more sense. Go ahead and do what resonates for you. There is no right or wrong, and no single solution is right for every couple. You are in charge of bringing your vision of sparkle into reality.

Relationship sparkle is the "erotic" of a relationship, not just the sexual energy and passion, but a broader idea. The erotic is the "it factor" of love which creates thrilling and adventurous experiences that give meaning to life. It is the antidote for the mundane of human existence, electric energy that is the difference between feeling fully alive rather than just living. A relationship "sparkles" when you share joyous experiences that make you feel vibrant, exhilarated, and loved, creating euphoria, fulfillment, and secure bonding. It's an intoxicating combination that will return you home to love!

Sparkling Point

Relationship sparkle is the erotic "it factor" of love; that which creates thrilling and adventurous experiences that give meaning to life. It is the antidote for the mundane of human existence. It is the electric energy that is the difference between feeling fully alive rather than just living.

Every relationship has sparkling moments at least some of the time. You create your own unique sparkle by putting energy into building on those moments that are exhilarating, unforgettable, and shine the most in your memories. Think of how you first became attracted to one another. How did you create fun and joy? Were you an adventurous, spirited, couple that played together, tried new things, and made each other laugh? Did you love travel, roller coasters, and polar bear plunges? Or, were you a couple that loved hiking, movies, museums, or simply hanging out on the couch together? There is no right or wrong, you are the best experts to know what brought the sparkle to your relationship.

Why have you lost your sparkle?

The more you focus your mental energy and actions on something, the more it becomes your reality, and so it is with relationships. If you focus on the details of problems and all that is wrong, that is what will manifest. If you lose your sparkle, you can become entrenched in boredom, restlessness, and loneliness. If you stay focused on creating sparkle, however, the spectacular, joyful aspects will grow. You must stay committed to keeping it going by taking action every single day.

Stuck in limiting beliefs

There are several reasons why you have lost your sparkle. The first is that you may be stuck in limiting beliefs that are preventing you from creating change. These beliefs true, they are simply myths that have grown popular in western culture over many generations. Given that negativity is a pervasive cultural perspective, it's understandable that the problem focus has seeped into beliefs about long-term love and encourages negative stories about the capacity for love to be everlasting. These myths do not serve you, rather they hinder you from believing that you can have a love that sparkles for a lifetime.

Sparkling Point

You have lost your sparkle because you are stuck in limiting beliefs that are preventing you from having hope that your relationship can change.

Here are examples of beliefs that may be holding you back:

Our situation is hopeless and serious.

We are broken and there is something wrong with us.

We don't have any sparkle in our relationship.

Change is too difficult.

We've been unhappy for so long, that the present and future cannot be any different.

We don't have a clue how to start to change.

It will take a long time for our relationship to heal and nothing will help us.

Our problems are too big to fix.

We have no energy to work on our relationship.

Change won't last.

Our problems are too big and too complicated.

The solutions to our problems seem too difficult.

There is nothing good about our relationship.

We don't have a clue how we will know if we can be fulfilled forever.

Debunking myths

The first step to prepare for creating sparkle is to debunk your limiting beliefs and create alternate beliefs that will serve you in moving forward. Changing limiting beliefs will help you to get out of your own way and start moving forward. Here are some alternate ideas that may empower you:

Your problems are not serious. They are simply misunderstandings and normal complaints of daily life that have many easy solutions.

Your relationship is not hopeless or broken, you are simply stuck in destructive patterns of interaction.

Every relationship has sparkling moments at least some of the time.

Your past does not dictate your present or your future. You already what to do, you lost track of it.

Change is not only possible; it is inevitable and can happen instantly.

All possible solutions are valid, even if they seem useless, ridiculous, or silly.

Small improvements can snowball into big, lasting change.

There are infinite possibilities for recreating sparkle.

Revert to old patterns is temporary. You can recover quickly.

Focusing on complaining, details of problems, and how they got that way is a waste of time.

Searching for and building solutions is much more useful and effective than problem solving.

There are solutions and exceptions for every problem.

Knowing what to avoid is just as important as knowing what to fix.

It is useful to search for differences that make a difference to you.

Stuck in relationship trash talk

One reason you may have lost your sparkle is that you are stuck in "relationship trash talk". Your mental energy, conversations and interactions are focused in the wrong direction. You are fixating on all that is wrong: verbalizing details of your problems and how they got that way. Speaking in negative terms is guaranteed to create more of what you don't want, focusing little to no energy on the sparkling moments.

Sparkling Point

Your mental energy, conversations, and interactions are focused in the wrong direction: on problems and how they got that way. You are diverting your focus off the sparkling moments.

When couples come for their first session of therapy, they are usually hell-bent on describing problems in detail. They lead with a "blame campaign"; accusing each other without acknowledging their own contribution to their problems. I hear story after story of miserable experiences and hate they have for one another, citing examples of constant fighting, explosiveness, silent treatment, and no sex. Instead of creating sparkle, precious energy is wasted on arguing over right and wrong, true or false, correct or incorrect. I've seen couples who have been stuck in these destructive, love-killing patterns for months, years, or even decades.

Sparkling Point

The more you stay stuck in "relationship trash talk", pouring all your verbal energy into problem-saturated talk, the bigger and more entrenched your problems will become.

The shift

According to motivational speaker Tony Robbins, you have to destroy your limiting beliefs, negative thoughts, and actions, and "stack the good." In the field of psychology the prevailing wisdom is that many mental health and physical problems are actually caused by patterns of negative thinking, worries, and destructive beliefs. There is proof that negative, worried thoughts actually get stuck in cells of the body and become the source of many diseases. Harmful, repetitive thoughts get wired into the brain and create feelings and behaviors that manifest the very thing you do not want. Negative words, beliefs, and actions can be the death knell of a relationship. That's why it is critical to shift away from limiting beliefs and trash talk. Believe it or not, you can create improvement without discussing your problems at all. Instead, pour your energy into the sparkle: imagining and creating moments that create joy, fun, closeness, fulfillment, thrill, passion, and well-being.

If you have ever watched a professional doubles tennis match you will see this concept in action. Doubles partners focus on their goal, what they are doing well, and support of one another. They never focus on what is going wrong, bad shots, or criticism. They stay resolved to support each other, regroup, and to build a new strategy after each point. Doubles partners focus on creating all new strategies in real time. After each point they huddle together, pat each other on the back, re-strategize and shout "Lets GO!"

I challenge you to be the best doubles team you can be and have relentless commitment to your shift! Keep your mental focus on getting back your sparkle, even if you get exhausted and hit bumps in the road. Let yourself go, dream, and tap into your ability to have vision of just how shimmering your relationship can be. Banish limiting thoughts and trash talk and remember problems are temporary, but the sparkle of love shines on forever!

Sparkling Point

Commit to saying no to negative thoughts and actions, and stack the good!

Stay relentlessly committed to keep your mental focus on the good and getting back your sparkle!

Turn trash talk into sparkling conversations

Words are powerful, and they can either be gifts of love or love-killing weapons. Once words are spoken they can never be taken back. Harsh words ruin sparkling moments, intimacy, and closeness. After all, words rooted in anger, rudeness, and disrespect are certainly not aphrodisiacs! Every word you say to your partner reveals how you feel about them. If you approach with critical, demeaning or abusive language, I guarantee your partner will shut down and have little desire to be near you. Ask yourself if your words convey love, respect, and kindness, or rudeness, disrespect, or lack of concern?

Sparkling Point

Words are powerful: they can either be gifts of love or love-killing weapons. Once words are spoken they can never be taken back, and they can do severe damage to loving feelings.

Seven steps to sparkling conversations

Sparkling conversations involve the use of compliments, shifting problems into solvable complaints, asking constructive questions, and searching for, observe, and predicting sparkle.

Step # 1 - Compliments

Most people love to hear nice things about themselves. A good starting point to transform relationship trash talk into sparkling conversation is to focus on compliments. Upon hearing a compliment, the unconscious opens up to what is coming next and creates a sense of affinity and respect for the teller of the words. When the unconscious hears repetitive negative complaining, however, it tends to shut down and avoids taking in that information. Some ways to begin conversations with compliments are:

"I'm so impressed with"…
"Thank you for doing"…
"I really appreciate when you"…
"I really like that you did"…
"I appreciate when you" …
"It's great when you"…..
"I feel happy when you"…..
"You are really great at"…
"I'm proud of you when you"…

Step # 2 - Shifting big problems into solvable complaints

Another negative communication pattern that couples are often stuck in is labeling their problems in huge, negative terms. Being vague about what you desire can be very confusing and prevent your partner from responding with reasonable solutions. Vague complaints such as "change your bad attitude", "improve your self–esteem", or "you are too detached" usually go nowhere. Since most people are not mind readers, you need to tell your partner in simple and clear language *exactly* what you want. It is most productive to redefine big problems into specific, solvable terms. Complaints are those things that concern or bother you, and yet have many possible solutions. Here are a few common examples of vague problem descriptions:

"You don't make me happy."
"You need better self-esteem."
"You're too controlling."
"You need to be a better person."
"You don't care about me."
"You're a nag."
"You don't make me feel loved."
"You're too needy."
"I don't trust you."
"You smother me."
"I don't feel close to you."
"You don't treat me right."

"You're never satisfied."
"You're checked out and cold."

It's very difficult to know where to begin to create solutions for big problems, and easy for the listener to get frozen in verbal paralysis. After thirty years as a couples' therapist, even I don't have a clue how to make someone have better self-esteem, be a better person, or make another person feel loved, though I certainly have ideas and interpretations about what those complaints usually mean.

Step # 3 - Constructive questions

Another tip for building sparkling conversations is to ask useful, constructive questions and avoid blaming, negative questions that are difficult to answer. Those questions put your partner on the defense and usually lead to poor outcomes. The more you question in blaming ways, the more your partner will likely fight back with defensiveness, attacking, and shutting down. "Why" questions and a blaming tone from a position of attack are also, destructive. Phrases such as "you always, you never, you should, you need to, you have to" evoke a desire to challenge back and escalate to prove points. There is no sparkle in those techniques! Here are a few examples of sparkling questions that open open up conversation and encourage solution building:

> "What do you need from me right now to make this better?"
> "What exactly can I do to make you feel loved and cared for?"
> "What will help you feel better about this situation right now?"
> "What specifically would be happening for you to feel closer to me?"
> "What am I doing that you would appreciate more of?"
> "How would you know if my self - esteem was better? What would I be doing differently?"
> "What do I need to do for you to consider me a better person?"
> "How would I be treating you if things were better?"
> "How will you know you can trust me, and what signs would you see?"
> "How will you know when my nagging has stopped?"
> "What am I doing when you feel I am tuned in rather than checked out and cold?"
> "What do you want me to start doing more or less of?"

Here are some suggested answers that contain the beginnings of sparkling conversations:

> "I'm happy when you take time to talk to me a little bit every day and give me hugs and kisses."
> "I feel cared for when you take the time to text me during the day."
> "I feel better when you share responsibility for chores and the kids without asking or waiting for me to tell you what to do."
> "I feel loved when you initiate sex."
> "I feel valued when you are affectionate without expecting sex."

"I feel loved when you cuddle with me without expecting sex."

"I listen best when you don't repeat yourself or follow me around."

"I like when you tell me something just once or twice."

"I need some time to be left alone and decompress when I come home from work."

"I don't like when you stay in the basement and watch TV by yourself all night."

"I don't like when you tell me what to wear or what to do."

Say what you want in assertive but kind, respectful words such as:

"I would really appreciate you to greet me in the morning and night with a hug and a kiss, and ask me and how my day was."

"I like hugs and kisses a few times a day."

"I would like to talk more at dinner with our cell phones turned off."

"I like more phone calls from you during the day."

"I like taking turns to plan fun dates together."

"I like when you make sexy moves during the day that might lead to sex later."

"I like being affectionate when we are not having sex."

"I like some time alone when I first come home from work."

"I need some time to myself to cool off when we are having a conflict."

"Please don't remind me after I have told you I will take care of a chore."

Sparkling Point

Use constructive questions to open up discussion of sparkling moments to build solutions and compromises.

Sparkling Point

Once you know what your partner wants, JUST DO IT! GIVE IT TO THEM!

Your partner shouldn't have to ask for what they want. Pay close attention to the specific actions your partner wants. Memorize them, keep written reminders if needed, and commit to implementing.

Step # 4 - Searching for sparkle: the exceptions to problems in the present, past, and future

Once you have begun to shift your beliefs and conversations away from a problem – saturated focus, the next step is to search for the sparkle in the exceptions to your problems. Exceptions are the times when complaints are not happening, all is going well, and sparkling moments are abundant. No problem happens 100% of the time, there is always some exception to the rule, even just a little bit! There are many examples that validate exceptions being present, even in difficult times.

Is an empty glass really empty, or are there other alternate perspectives? If the volume in the glass is half, do you see it as half empty or half full? Even a glass that looks completely empty is full of air. Can you envision that glass of air connected to the air in the universe as a bigger possibility? Also consider the Chinese philosophy of yin and yang: the belief that two opposing forces exist in the world that are complementary parts of each other. The yin is the negative, dark side, and the yang is the positive, bright side. So it is with relationships: every yin has its yang, and there is always another side. Where you place your mental focus and conversation creates more of what you do or don't want. What do you choose: the yin or the yang, the dark or the light, half empty or half full?

Step # 5 - Pay attention to the sparkle in your present, past and future

Observing and keeping track of the sparkle that is already happening can help you track and locate more of what you want. Observe your interactions for at least a week. Focus not on the details of complaints or what is wrong, instead focus on the sparkling good times that make a difference. Search in your present, future, and past, and identify specific behaviors and who does what differently. Ask yourself what you already know how to do that you can bring forward into the present and begin to do more of right now.

I often find that couples are actually doing much better than they realize. Sometimes they are so locked into wanting to vent about not doing well, that they miss the sparkle. They zero in on one conflict that happened during the week, and unless I guide them, they may argue for the entire session about one small conflict. When I ask, "When you consider the entire week since you were here, how many days were good?" I often find they are surprised to realize conflict has decreased significantly, and 90% of the week was peaceful and happy.

If you are having difficulty finding sparkle in your present, search your past. Your past is useful because it holds within it a rich collection of sparkling moments, successes, and exceptions to your problems. If you once had sparkling times, the memory of those still exists in your unconscious. Was there a time in the past when you felt more content and fulfilled? Be careful not to backslide into ruminating about the details of past problems. You can also access useful memories from the past by meditating on those times. Allow yourself to sit in a quiet space for a time when you don't need to do anything else.

Concentrate on returning to experiences with your partner. Some questions to contemplate:

> Why were you initially attracted to one another?
> What did you find appealing about your partner?
> What did you enjoy doing together?
> How did you build your friendship and companionship?
> What experiences did you share that were the most fun for the two of you?
> Did you have lively discussions about interesting topics?

Were you curious about each other's goals and dreams?

Did you have fulfilling affection and sexual intimacy?

Was there mutual tuning in to one another, openness, and initiation?

Sparkling Point

Your past is useful because it holds within it a rich collection of your sparkling moments, successes, and exceptions to your problems as well as clues to the possible sparkling moments you can create now and in your future.

Many couples are often surprised by how much sparkle there actually was in their past. One way to access those useful memories is to use the mantra technique of thanking yourself before you go to sleep at night for remembrance of sparkling times you had in the past. Upon waking in the morning, invite and welcome in creative ideas for more sparkle, good memories, and potential solutions. Your unconscious will take these clues literally and go to work excavating past sparkling moments and bringing them into your consciousness. You already know what to do to create more good times. Trust that information is stored in your unconscious, and with prompts, will bring the sparkle forward in new creative ways.

Sparkling Point

You already know what to do to create more sparkling moments. Trust that useful information from the past is stored in your unconscious memory. With prompts, it will bring the past sparkle forward into the present in new creative ways.

Sparkling Point

Your unconscious holds the memories of past sparkling times and successes. You have not forgotten them, you have simply stored them away in your unconscious mind. You can retrieve them and bring them forward into your present and future.

Another source of useful information is to project to a future of sparkling moments. Visualize what already will have happened in a successful, fulfilled future. Imagine yourself at a point in your future when your problems have been solved. You wake up one morning to discover a video has been posted about your relationship and it has gone viral overnight. Picture exactly what is happening in that video. Visualize how you and your partner are interacting differently.

Sparkling Point

Your creative vision of your future also holds clues to creating sparkling moments and solutions in your present. By pretending your problems are miraculously gone, you can skip over problem details and start creating a happy present in your imagination. Then take action to make it happen in real time.

Project yourself into a happy fulfilling future with sparkling moments and problems solved. Your creative vision of your future also holds clues to creating sparkling moments and solutions in your present. By pretending your problems are miraculously gone, you can skip over problem details and start creating a happy present in your imagination. Then take action to make it happen in real time.

Step #6 - Predict sparkle, change, and improvement every day.

Another way to create sparkling moments and solutions is to predict them in the present. Each morning, take a few moments to contemplate and write down a prediction about whether you are going to have a good day or a bad day. Visualize yourself in the evening saying, "This was a really amazing day for us. I felt happy because…" or "today was sparkling because …", then focus on the positive interactions that would have already happened that day. Email or text your prediction to yourself and your partner, or write it on a slip of paper, and place it somewhere you will notice when you return home. Take a few moments later in the evening to think back over your prediction, your day, and the outcome. Discuss with your partner whether your guess was accurate or not. If you had a great, sparkling-moment day, or even just a good day, even just a little bit, discuss the positives in detail. If it was a so-so or bad day, do not spend time talking about the details of what went wrong. Instead, search for and discuss different actions you both could have taken that would have made it a better day.

Running this prediction check each morning will help you tune into the specifics of your sparkling days, the differences between the good times and the bad times, and what you both can do to make a positive difference. Prediction suggests to your unconscious the distinct possibility of a sparkling, great, or good day. Most people don't predict bad days. Why would you want to put any energy into creating an unhappy outcome?

Step #7 - Do one thing different

Hopefully you are practicing, observing, and searching for sparkling moments and exceptions, and keeping your words and conversations constructive. If you find you are not making much progress yet, you may not be putting your energy into actions that make a difference. It's inevitable that previous problematic patterns may resurface from time to time because relationship styles, patterns, and coping mechanisms run very deep in the gut. I don't believe they can be completely eradicated, but they can be minimized as new skills become habit. The goal is to minimize these old messages and patterns, practice new skills, and transform them into constructive habits.

If you are still stuck, another useful play is to do one thing different. You don't need to understand what is wrong or exactly what is causing your problems. Responding to problems with new responses, doing the opposite, or changing your location can interrupt previous patterns. The next time you have a disagreement, try responding in a different or opposite way. Your strategy does not have to fit the problem or the argument, it can just be a difference of any kind. You may even try a funny or surprising response. The goal is to find differences that make a difference. This strategy may also help you discern what is most useful and least useful in breaking patterns.

I've been very impressed with the creative and sometimes humorous solutions many couples have utilized while attempting to do one thing different. Some have used the strategy of hugs and tickling if they anticipate an argument. Others have used funny cue words and mantras to break tensions while some have committed to a 24-hour break to manage themselves, then return to solution-build when both are calm. Taking a break can result in a useful change in perspective, and in doing so, you may find the problem was not worth discussion.

Sparkling Point

When old problem patterns or conflicts surface, try doing something different, surprising, or funny.

You may have been trapped in a pattern of problem-saturated thinking, complaining, and negative interactions for a long time. Those habits will undoubtedly resurface from time to time. You may automatically drift back into a negative pattern of ruminating about problems and getting stuck in arguing about the details of what's wrong. It's a good idea to monitor yourselves for these ten obstacles that may drag you back into destructive habits:

Ten obstacles to creating sparkle

> Losing your solution focus and getting stuck in a problem - saturated focus.
> Getting stuck in relationship trash talk.
> Staying stuck in solutions that don't make a difference.
> Failing to interrupt negative conversations and patterns of behavior.
> Your goals that are too vague and unmanageable.
> Forgetting to cooperate with each other by receiving and giving.
> Repeating destructive arguments and conversations.
> Forgetting to check in about what differences make a difference.
> Failing to monitor your progress.
> Failing to keep progress moving forward into consistent habits.

In this chapter, we've discussed the critical importance of shifting away from problems and how they got that way, turning your focus towards all that is possible, developing new limitless beliefs, creating sparkling conversations, and searching for sparkle in your present, future, and past. The plays that follow are designed to help you start practicing various ways to build sparkling solutions and exceptions to your problems.

Sparkling Point

You have been given the gift of a relationship with a loving partner! With tender cherishing and consistent action, light up your love with sparkling moments!

❖ PLAY # 11

Undoing Limiting Beliefs

Limiting beliefs are not truths. They are nothing more than entrenched ideas that send you on a destructive path and become habit. These assumptions are distorted, irrational, and do not support the health and growth of a relationship. Over time they transform into automatic thoughts that impact your interactions with your partner.

Limiting beliefs can be shifted and decreased by creating new beliefs that are more useful and lead you to constructive conversation and solution building.

On one side of the page, list the limiting beliefs and thoughts that are holding you back in your relationship. On the other side of the page, create alternate beliefs about your relationship that will serve you better and move you towards growth and improvement.

Choose one belief that feels the most critical to you as a starting point for change.

Discuss with your partner:

Play # 11

Takeaway Notes

❖ PLAY # 12

Words are Magic

Your words have power. They can either be magical gifts of love or love-killing weapons. In this play, begin by contemplating the messages you are conveying to your partner. Is your overall tone one of respect, kindness, and compassion, or of rudeness, disrespect, and harshness? The latter is the "trash talk" that destroys love and can cause permanent damage to a relationship. In this play, you will practice transforming trash talk into sparkling conversations.

Step # 1 Compliment! Compliment! Compliment!

A good starting point is to focus on compliments and appreciation. Take some time to write ways you can express compliments and appreciation to your partner. Start with these phrases:

I'm so impressed with......

Thank you for doing....

I really appreciate when you......

Step # 2 Shift big problems into small, solvable complaints

Describing problems in vague, negative terms makes it difficult for your partner to respond in a productive way that can lead to solutions and compromises. It is helpful to redefine big problems as more positive complaints with specific words that lead to productive conversation. Keep it short and tell your partner the particulars of what bothers you and what you want.

Write down the words, phrases, and sentences you are currently using to describe your concerns and upsets to your partner:

1.

2.

3.

4.

5.

6.

7.

8.

9.

10.

Now re-state each description with new words and keep it as simple and clear as possible. I suggest only one or two sentences to describe what is bothering you, and the same for what you want. Here are some ways to begin:

Problem Description

I am really upset about….

I am feeling hurt because….

I am concerned about….

I'm troubled by….

I would really appreciate…

Could you please……

I respectfully ask you to….

Can you please do more of….

Step # 3 Constructive questions

Another way to build sparkling conversations is to ask useful, constructive questions and avoid blaming or negative questions that shut down conversation. Once you've been given clear specifics about your partner's wishes and needs, start paying attention to opportunities to give your partner exactly what they have asked for. Make sure you commit those actions to your memory, because your partner shouldn't have to keep asking for what they want. Write answers to the questions below.

When is…. (the complaint/problem) not happening?

Exactly when, where, and how is this happening?

What are you each doing differently at those times?

What am I already doing, even if only a little bit, that can be helpful to you?

What do you need from me right now to make this better?

What exactly can I do to make you feel loved and cared for?

What will help you feel better about this situation right now?

Specifically, what would be happening for you to feel closer to me?

How would you know if my self-esteem were better?

What would I be doing differently?

What do I need to do for you to consider me a better person?

How would I be treating you if things were better?

How will you know you can trust me, and what signs would you see?

How will you know when my nagging has stopped?

What am I doing when you feel I am tuned in rather than checked out and cold?

What do you want me to start doing more of, and stop doing?

Play # 12

Takeaway Notes

❖ **PLAY # 13**

Miracles on the Way

Miracles can sneak up to you quietly and sit down next to you. They may also be dropped on you like a ton of bricks! Do you believe in miracles, coincidences, or unexplainable experiences? You may believe these are from God, the Universe, the collective unconscious, another spiritual source, your own unconscious sense of knowing, or your ability to manifest what you want. I believe there is something bigger than we mortals know, and the spectacular can happen, sometimes instantly.

For this play, the task is to imagine miracle solutions for your current relationship struggles. I ask you to suspend doubt, limitations, and disbeliefs. Let yourself create the details of your miracle: dream it, imagine it, and let it flow out of you. Trust that you already know what you want and how to get it. Trust that your miracle is already on the way to you!

You may find it helpful to audiotape yourself reading the instructions below, then relax and listen to it. Take a few moments to sit quietly by yourself in a comfortable position. Focus on slowing down your breathing and begin to relax all of your muscles.

Say to yourself, "I am letting it all settle".

When you feel completely relaxed, begin to whisper the following to yourself three times:

Thank you for the miracles and solutions I am about to receive.

I invite in growth and improvement.

Now place your mental focus on the following:

Suppose when you go to sleep tonight, a miracle occurs. When you awaken the next morning, your relationship is now in the most joyous, fulfilling state you can possibly imagine. Your issues, concerns, trouble, conflict, and differences are now miraculously gone. Allow yourself to visualize the details of your miracle. Focus specifically on what is happening and who is doing what differently. What differences are making a difference to you? Sit with your miracle for as long as you wish. Allow it to take shape and form as it will from your own creativity and intuition. When you are ready, in your own time, come back to the room to orient yourself to the place you are sitting, and allow yourself a few moments to flutter your eyes open.

You may wish to do this play with your partner or do it individually. Another option is to jot down your experience, what you saw, what you felt, and how the experience affected you. Then find a time to sit with your partner, hold hands, describe the miracle solutions you envisioned, and share your takeaways from this play.

Questions for your contemplation:

What can you take away from your miracle visualization that you can begin to do right now?

Ask your partner what they most want from the miracle experience?

What are you willing to give to meet their desires?

It is now your partner's turn to give to you.

Ask yourselves what is the easiest to do right now?

Give each other a hug.

Now take some time to complete the following either separately or together:

All Possible Sparkle List

In two columns list the numbers 1 to 50 and write down every sparkle and solution that has come to mind after doing your miracle visualization. Allow yourself to stretch your imagination and empty your brain of all possible ideas. Do not edit yourself. You might think of experiences, actions and responses you have never tried before. Don't give up if you don't reach fifty. Just try your best and let your creativity flow.

1.   26.

2.   27.

3.   28.

4.   29.

5.   30.

6.   31.

7.   32.

8.   33.

9.   34.

10.   35.

11.	36.
12.	37.
13.	38.
14.	39.
15.	40.
16.	41.
17.	42.
18.	43.
19.	44.
20.	45.
21.	46.
22	47.
23.	48,
24.	49.
25.	50.

Share your list of all possible sparkle with your partner. Search through the lists and choose the top ten ideas you both like the most.

1.

2.

3.

4.

5.

6.

7.

8.

9.

10.

Now choose your top three:

Choose your top idea that you find the easiest to do, and discuss the actions you are each willing to take.

Play # 13

Takeaway Notes

❖ **PLAY # 14**

Searching for Buried Sparkle

Once you have begun to shift your beliefs, conversations, and actions away from problems, your next step is to search for the sparkle: the exceptions to your problems.

Observe and pay attention to the sparkle in your present, past, and future

Pay attention and start observing the sparkle that is already happening, going well, and you want more of. Observe your interactions with your partner for at least a week. Focus not on the details of complaints or what is wrong, but on the times you felt joy, loved, and fulfilled. Search for sparkle in your present, future, and past. Think of specifics and what you and your partner are doing differently. Consider what you already know that you can bring forward into the present and do more of right now. Search in your past for happy memories of sparkle. List your top ten happiest moments as a couple so far:

1.

2.

3.

4.

5.

6.

7.

8.

9.

10.

List all versions of sparkle you either observe in the present, remember from the past, or can imagine happening in the future:

Predicting sparkle

You can also take some unpredictable and surprising actions to raise more sparkle to the surface. In this play, the focus is on predicting sparkle in the present, doing something different, and creating sneaky surprises. These activities are vague in order to allow your creative mind to discover sparkle that you may not have noticed before, especially if you are having difficulty finding it, or are confused about why it shows up and why it doesn't.

Each morning, take a few moments to contemplate and write down a prediction about whether your day will be sparkling, or "so - so". Visualize yourself at the end of the day by saying to yourself:

This was a really amazing sparkling day for us because....

I felt happy today because......

Today was sparkling because ......

Focus on the positive interactions that would have already happened that day. Email or text your prediction to yourself and your partner, or write it on a slip of paper, fold it up, and place it somewhere that you will notice when you return home. Take a few moments later in the evening to think back over your day, your prediction, and the outcome.

Discuss with your partner whether your guess was accurate or not. If you had a so-so or bad day, do not spend time talking about its details. Instead, discuss different actions you both could have taken to make it a good or great sparkling day.

Do one thing different

Another useful play is to "do something different". You don't need to understand what is going wrong, and your attempted solutions do not need "fit" your problems. New interactions, doing the opposite, or even changing your environment can break old patterns. The next time you have disagreement, try responding in an unexpected or opposite way than you have ever done before. Your strategy does not need to fit the problem or the argument, it can just be different, funny, or surprising. You are looking for new differences that have an impact and make a difference. This strategy may help you discern what is most useful in solving conflicts.

Every day for one week, try doing one thing different that will benefit your relationship. May be as simple as a hug and kiss at the beginning of an argument, changing your location of where you argue, or doing something humorous that is unrelated to the problem at hand. Keep a log of the different activities you try.

Do One Thing Different Log

Monday:

Tuesday:

Wednesday:

Thursday:

Friday:

Saturday:

Sunday:

Examine your list and decide which actions made a difference to you and your partner: Which of these actions do you and your partner desire to increase?

Sneaky surprises

Now that you have learned how to search for sparkle in your present, past, and future, predict sparkle, and do one thing different, use all of that information to bring on a "sneak attack" to your partner. Keep a list of ways you can surprise your partner with sparkling moments. Let your creative juices flow and don't edit yourself. Keep track of which sneaky surprises resonate the most with your partner.

Play # 14

Takeaway Notes

CHAPTER 4

Sparkling Points Summary

Relationship sparkle is the erotic "it factor" of love that creates thrilling and adventurous experiences that enhance your life. It is the antidote for the mundane of human existence and the electric energy that is the difference between being fully alive rather than just living.

If you have lost your sparkle, you may be because you are stuck in limiting beliefs that prevent you from having hope, your relationship can change.

Your mental energy, conversations, and interactions may be focused on problems and how they got that way. You have taken the focus away from the sparkling moments of your relationship. The more you stay stuck pouring your verbal energy into "problem-saturated talk', the more entrenched your problems become. You have to say NO to your negative thoughts and actions, and stack the good!

Words are powerful. They can either be gifts of love or love-killing weapons. Using sparkling words and language leads to more sparkle, doable, concrete solutions, and actions. Complaints you articulate should be specific, small, and understandable.

Use constructive questions to further open up your discussion of sparkling moments, building solutions, and gold standards.

Your partner shouldn't have to ask for what they want. Pay close attention to the specific needs your partner expresses, memorize them, keep written reminders if needed, and commit to implementing.

Your past is useful because it holds a rich collection of your past sparkling moments, successes, and exceptions to your problems.

Your creative vision of the future also holds clues to creating sparkling moments and solutions in your present. By pretending your problems are miraculously gone, you can skip problem details and start imagining a happy present.

When old problem patterns or conflicts surface, try doing something, anything different, surprising, or funny.

CHAPTER 5

Going for Gold

Words of Wisdom

Talking becomes the primary tool to spin the straw of problems into the gold of exceptions, solutions, and ultimately a more satisfying life.

- Insoo Kim Berg and Yvonne Dolan, authors of Tales of Solutions

We are totally responsible for ourselves. We cannot look for reasons outside of us. Still, we are forever blaming outside forces for our feelings and actions, seldom asking, "Why am I choosing to act or react that way?" Happiness and true freedom come only when we assume full responsibility for who and what we are. As long as we feel comfortable putting blame on others, we will never be required to evaluate and change our own behaviors.

- Leo Buscaglia, author of Loving Each Other

If there is bitterness in the heart, sugar in the mouth won't make life sweeter.

- Yiddish Proverb

As selfishness and complaint pervert the mind, so love with its joy clears and sharpens the vision.

- Helen Keller

CHAPTER 5

Going for Gold

The low road or the high road?

As the old English proverb says, familiarity breeds contempt, but I believe it's not familiarity or length of time together that depletes relationships of their sparkle. Love dies when couples lower their standards. Relationships usually begin with the best possible intentions, what I call the "gold standard" phase. If you are attracted and interested in pursuing someone, you usually want to make a good impression by putting your best foot forward. New dating situations are usually characterized by high levels of respect, kindness, interest, thoughtfulness, generosity, and intimacy.

Why do gold standards deteriorate as time goes by? The answer is that many of us do not grow up learning healthy relationship skills. Instead, we carry forward from childhood harmful behaviors that destroy love. Couples stop nurturing their relationship by ceasing to put consistent energy and action into maintaining their original standards. When this happens, disrespect, defensiveness, uncontrolled anger, retaliation, explosiveness, and silent treatment creep into the relationship.

Sparkling Point

It's not familiarity or length of time that depletes relationships of their sparkle. It's because couples lower their standards and replace them with destructive, unloving habits.

If you have lost the gold standards you had in the beginning, you may wonder how you will ever heal the damage that has accumulated over the years. If you are a new couple who may have gotten off to a negative or mediocre start, perhaps you are wondering if you can find a way to create better standards, or if you're simply not a match. But no matter how long you and your partner have been stuck in dysfunction, there is hope you can improve your standards and even boost them to gold. At times I have been pleasantly surprised by couples who seem to be well on their way to divorce step up and create high quality standards. Some grasp the process quickly and make major changes in one session. Others need a few weeks, months, or a year or two. Sadly, I have also seen couples who, despite a foundation of gold standards, inflict so much damage over the years that there is no way to recover.

Sparkling Point

No matter how long you and your partner have been stuck in dysfunction, there is hope you can improve your standards and even boost them to gold!

The seven deadly love killers

In order to rebuild your gold standards, it's important to first understand what interactions to avoid. The seven deadly love killers are destructive, unproductive ways you interact and respond to one another. They are small, daily habits that are repeated thousands of times and transform into negative interactional patterns.

Sparkling Point

A love killer is any action or lack of action that your partner experiences as upsetting, hurtful, disrespectful, or unloving.

Love Killer #1 – Disrespect

"He *always* screams at me and calls me disgusting names. It makes me feel abused and I *never* do anything to deserve it. There's nothing I can do to get him to stop because he simply ignores me if I'm upset."

"Nag, nag, nag, she orders me around like I'm a two-year old, and gets into my business like she owns me or is my mother. She's controlling and our problems are her fault. I stopped listening a long time ago, and now I just do whatever I want."

"He acts like a tyrant, demanding everything be on his terms: from big things to little things. My needs never matter. I feel like he's trying to control my happiness."

"Her tone is always rude, with eye rolling and talking under her breath, I can't take it anymore."

These statements are common examples of the disrespect couples routinely report to me in therapy. Unfortunately, disrespect is an epidemic in today's world. The gold standards many couples established when they began dating often transform into the ugliness of disrespect and mistreatment. After years of conflict, anger often transmutes into rage, and love dies.

Sparkling Point

Disrespect is the #1 killer of loving feelings. When it is allowed to fester, mutual respect and civility suffer greatly. Disrespect includes any verbal, non-verbal, or physical action that is harsh, unkind, or demeaning.

I have a very broad definition of disrespect, and I hold myself to that gold standard in both my professional and personal lives. Obvious forms of verbal disrespect include screaming, cursing, and name-calling terms like stupid, jerk, idiot, crazy, psycho, bitch, asshole, or worse. Physical forms include storming out; slamming, breaking, or throwing things, pushing, hitting, and intimidating. These actions can easily cross the line of disrespect into emotional and physical abuse. But more subtle behaviors can be just as hurtful and abusive. Rolling your eyes in disgust, a rude tone, wagging your finger in someone's face, whispering derogatory remarks, cursing under your breath, mocking, ignoring, silent treatment, and refusing to make eye contact are all forms of disrespect.

You may think that the more subtle ways of acting out anger mentioned won't do any real damage. However, they *will* get noticed, not only by your partner, but also by your children. When you've been with a partner a long time, it's normal to reach the end of your rope more quickly than when you first got together. Yes, you are only human, and anger and frustration are given in all relationships. It's normal for voice tone and volume to go up a bit in the heat of anger. But letting yourself get out of control and escalating into rage gives your partner the message that you don't value or respect them as a human being, let alone as a partner.

Sparkling Point

If you are letting disrespect run rampant and invading your partner's emotional and physical boundaries, you are putting your relationship at risk. Over time it *will* chip away at respect, trust, and closeness.

It's obviously hurtful to be on the receiving end of disrespect, but being the giver does emotional harm as well. It might make you feel better in the moment to scream and lash out in rage, but consider the guilt and shame you may feel afterwards. All forms of disrespect, direct or subtle, verbal or physical, send demeaning messages such as: "You are not worthy of my respect, I don't value you, I don't care how I treat you, and I don't care how much I hurt you." Are these messages you want to send to the person you love? The other victims are the observers: your children and grandchildren. By witnessing disrespect, they learn that an angry free-for-all is an okay way to treat someone you love.

Sparkling Point

Your relationship is the blueprint for your children's future, and each time you cross over into disrespect, you emotionally damage your partner, yourself, and everyone else around you.

Though this may be difficult to accept and understand, you are in charge of how your partner treats you. Each time you fail to react to disrespect, you give your partner permission to continue to mistreat you. It's your job to be clear about the gold standard of respect you require. I'm not suggesting that you are responsible for your partner's disrespectful behaviors. You *are,* however, responsible for allowing your partner to treat you poorly. An important question for you to contemplate is: why have you allowed disrespect to become acceptable in your relationship? Think back to when you first met your partner and visualize those early dating days. Can you recall how you treated one other and the good feelings at that time?

In the beginning most of us want to impress each other and be respectful at all times. When you argued, you may have worked diligently to hold it together because you didn't want to make a bad impression or lose a potential mate. How long do you think your relationship would have lasted if you had lower standards at that time and called each other names, cursed, screamed, gotten intimidating, or even physical? What if you had made derogatory comments, or become physically intimidating or even abusive? If your potential partner had any self-respect, you would've been dumped, pronto! When couples eventually reach the point of making a commitment, it often brings with it a sense of well-being and emotional security. But as reassuring as that may be, unfortunately, it can also be a turning point when disrespect begins to fester and partners stop caring about how they treat one other.

Think about how you conduct yourself in the outside world. You probably abide by socially acceptable standards and treat others with respect, whether it's with colleagues, bosses, or friends. How successful do you think you would be in those situations if you routinely ranted, name called, or got physically threatening? You probably would get fired, and your friends would ditch you, rightfully so. if you treated each other with civility and high regard at one time, you *can* re-create a new gold standard of respect and return to loving feelings. If you're realizing that you never had a high standard of respect, it's never too late to begin to create it now. Maintaining a gold standard of respect is not optional. It's critical to the health and well-being of your relationship, and each of you as individuals.

Sparkling Point

You are in charge of how your partner treats you. Each time you accept disrespect, you give your partner silent permission to continue to treat you that way.

Three steps to reset respect

You can spin the straw of disrespect into the gold standard of respect in three steps: defining respect and disrespect, committing to a completely respectful relationship, and identifying specific actions.

Step # 1: Define respect and disrespect and commit to staying respectful at all times. Respect is treating someone with consistent high regard and civility, both verbally and in actions.

Talking about your specific definitions, expectations, and beliefs about respect is an important conversation. Although the ways we define respect and disrespect in society are commonly agreed upon, those words may have very different meanings for different couples. For example, some partners consider looking each other in the eyes while speaking as the utmost sign of respect. Others consider eye contact during a conflict to be a sign of disrespect. Silence may indicate respect or perceived as passive-aggressive anger. Even in your worst moments, maintaining respect for one another will ensure that any message will be easy to give and receive, even the most painful. I'm not suggesting that you stuff your feelings and go silent. Anger and frustration are a normal part of human nature. We all have moments of feeling provoked and need limits about what we are willing to tolerate. Some common examples of respectful behaviors are:

Containing anger to an acceptable level

Keeping voice tone low and without attitude

Avoiding demeaning and derogatory words and name-calling

Making requests instead of giving orders

Using appropriate expression of upset feelings

Avoiding name-calling or demeaning comments

Exhibiting eye contact during conversation and disagreements

Staying physically and emotionally present during conflict

Respecting each other's physical space and boundaries

Step #2: Delete disrespect from your daily life.

Once you clearly define respect and disrespect, pay attention to your partner's definitions, and commit to staying within those guidelines. Do not under any circumstances let disrespect into your relationship. It often surfaces in the heat of conflict when you may be most vulnerable and say or do things that you later regret. But nothing good comes from making derogatory remarks and allowing anger to escalate. It's better to step away than to cause emotional harm to yourself and your partner. If you do step away, however, make sure you tell your partner you are doing so, and tell that you will reconnect when you are calmer.

Step #3: Build a gold standard of respectful boundaries.

An important part of the gold standard of respect is setting and respecting healthy boundaries. As an adult you have the right to determine what you are willing to receive from your partner. You should set boundaries for your own behavior as well, committing to managing yourself. Your partner does not have the right to intrude beyond your boundaries, and that goes two ways. It's important to take a firm stand and make it clear that disrespect is never acceptable, and you will not participate in it.

You also have the right to decide how to respond to your partner when they make a request of you. Whether you say yes or no, your partner needs to respect that decision. Likewise, if your partner says no to you or needs space, respect their decision as well. Saying *yes* as much as possible is an important part of being a giving, loving partner. The more you say yes and give what your partner wants, the less you will transgress each other's boundaries and the more you will limit conflict.

Sparkling Point

You can guarantee respect by committing to a gold standard of respecting yourself and giving and receiving only considerate communications. The deadly love killer triad: defensiveness, uncontrolled anger, and passive aggressive retaliation.

The "love killer triad": defensiveness, uncontrolled anger, and passive aggressive retaliation is a triple threat of harm to a relationship. Conflict is an extremely uncomfortable experience for many couples. Most of us do not grow up with positive views of conflict or the skills to productively resolve differences. The most common responses I hear from couples are what I call "the deadly trio of love killers": defensiveness, uncontrolled anger, and passive-aggressive retaliation. These are usually used in tandem, and are a hard habit to break. Using these responses usually increases conflict and result in issues festering without resolution or compromise, only to rise up again, as bigger monsters to slay.

Every human relationship has conflict some of the time. Unfortunately, conflict has gotten a bad reputation, almost always carrying negative connotations and assumptions that conflict is always destructive, leads to arguing and fighting, and that it is better to avoid it at all costs. The goal is not to completely remove conflict in your relationship, in fact; that is not possible. Every human carries within them perspectives, and opinions that rarely match completely with a partner. The goal is to understand one another's perspectives by listening, truly hearing, compromising, and building solutions together, even if the solution is to agree to disagree for now.

When couples are stuck in conflict cycles and emotions are raging out of control, I know one or both partners are waging a battle that has nothing to do with their partner. We carry within us the blueprint of experiences and responses from childhood. As children we lack the power or cognitive ability to respond to conflict in mature adult ways. The responses we have in our younger years are silence, lashing out, defensiveness, or passive-aggressive retaliation. When you get triggered by an experience in adulthood that is similar to one you faced as a child; it is natural to automatically use childhood responses. However, in adulthood these responses are usually destructive. As an adult you have the capability to listen, understand, compromise, offer solutions, and set healthy boundaries.

Love Killer # 2 - Defensiveness

"BUT I didn't …BUT I never…"BUT you always…BUT…BUT you never…BUT what about what you did?" Sound familiar? Repeated use of the word "BUT" is a sure sign you are stuck in defensiveness: a strategy used to avoid accountability for your own behavior. It presents as blaming your partner and refusing to receive feedback about yourself. The goal of defensiveness is to win by proving you are right and your partner is wrong. Playing this game is a sign that you're not listening to your partner's needs, and you are primarily interested in proving your point.

Sparkling Point

Defensiveness is any action used to avoid accepting responsibility for your own behavior and receiving feedback from your partner about how they experience you.

Defensiveness is a strategy children use when they are in the stage of learning right from wrong and are too immature to accept responsibility for their own misbehaviors. It's a common coping technique used to try to cover up naughty actions and avoid consequences. If you're a parent, think about how many times your kids have tried the "BUT I didn't do it" strategy on you. Is it ever effective, and how does it make you feel towards them? Are you more likely to resolve the issue productively if they're using a full-scale defensive strategy or if they acknowledge, apologize, and offer a solution?

In therapy sessions with children, I often ask if defensive pleading makes the situation better or worse, gets them out of trouble, or gets them what they want. Ninety-nine percent of the time they say: "NO, I usually end up getting in more trouble than I was already in." I ask: "So why do you keep doing something that doesn't work most of the time, gets you less of what you want, and gets you in more trouble?" After a deer in headlights moment, they usually giggle and realize defensiveness usually makes things much worse.

Think back to the childhood coping style that you used when you misbehaved and got into trouble. What defense was your strategy of choice: long-winded stories, pleading rationales, or "but I didn't" to plead your case? Take a moment to answer the following questions:

What was your strategy when you were in trouble as a kid? Were you a defensive pleader, "rationalizer", story teller, or tantrum thrower?

How have you transferred that behavior into your adult relationship? Does it work?

How do you feel if your partner does it to you?

Do you think it is helpful or harmful to your relationship?

Does it make sense to keep doing something that doesn't work and makes things worse?

Sparkling Point

Defensiveness makes conflict last longer and is a lose-lose strategy that solves nothing and creates distance and misunderstanding.

Love Killer #3: Uncontrolled Anger

Uncontrolled anger and attacks are the constant companions of disrespect and defensiveness. When combined, these three can become even more deadly. If you go into uncontrolled attack mode, you're allowing anger to escalate into overdrive and highjack your rational brain. It's a strategy to shut down conversation by using emotional, verbal, or physical intimidation, losing control with verbal aggression, physical posturing, and intimidation are emotional violence. This includes yelling, screaming, name-calling, cursing, door slamming, throwing things, making verbal threats, ranting, intimidating through voice tone, closing in on someone's physical space, approaching with intimidation, shoving, scratching, or swinging. These responses are remnants of childhood acting out and coping. If you allow yourself to be a receiver of out of control anger, you are giving your partner the message that emotional abuse is permissible. *No one should accept emotional abuse in any relationship, period.*

After long periods of mistreatment, a partner may finally stand up and say, "No more, I've had enough, I'm done with your attacks, and this relationship." In therapy sessions, I don't allow out of control ranting or any form of disrespect. Research tells us that uncontrolled anger can actually cause physical illness. If you're routinely out of control, you may be increasing your chances of heart attacks, strokes, or another hypertensive condition. If you're the receiver/victim of someone's intense anger over a long period of time, you are also putting your health at risk for depression, anxiety, panic attacks, and hypertension.

Sparkling Point

Lashing out with any form of uncontrolled anger and attacking your partner is emotional abuse. It harms everyone involved: the giver, the receiver, and the observers: your children.

Love Killer # 4: Passive - Aggressive Retaliation

Passive aggressive retaliation is any covert way a partner invades another person's boundaries to express anger and punish. Kids often lash out secretly because it makes them feel powerful, in control, and one up on their parents. If you were sneaky, secretive, passive aggressive, and unable to express your feelings in childhood, it's likely you may be using that coping style and acting out the same way in adulthood, though passive aggressive retaliation only makes things worse. Staying silent and saving up feelings usually backfires and results in more conflict, bigger explosions, and uncontrollable rage. Such behavior resolves nothing; and serves only to build mistrust, hostility, and emotional distance.

Defeating the love killers: effective conflict repair

Step #1: Manage yourself

You are responsible for your part in conflict repair and resolution. This first step is a to commit to managing your anger until you can engage in constructive conversation and productively build solutions with your partner. No matter what your partner does, lashing out or retaliating is *never* acceptable. When you feel anger on the rise, try these steps to get yourself in control.

Step # 2: Step away from conflict with respect.

Many couples get stuck in a pattern of fleeing from conflicts in a state of rage, abandoning one another, leaving conflict unresolved, and allowing painful feelings to fester. Walking away from conflict is not a failure, nor does it mean you are giving up on reaching a resolution. If you do it respectfully, it's actually a great strategy for cooling off, and it's much better to step away than to lash out.

If you decide it's getting heated and it's time to exit, do not storm out screaming and slamming doors. Instead, state clearly to your partner why you are stepping away. Return *only* when you are calm enough to re-engage in rational conversation. If you try a comeback and your anger begins to escalate, step away again. When you're able to stay calm, tell your partner why you're upset and what you need to resolve the conflict and heal the hurt feelings. Keep it short and do not repeat yourself. Get to resolution as quickly as possible and let it go. Here are some ways to say you need to exit:

> "I'm not going to fight like this because it's not good for us and it will just cause hurt."
> "I'm sorry you are so upset. I'm upset too, so let's take a break until we're both calmer."
> "I'm so upset that I don't feel I can stay here with you. I'm taking a break to cool off."
> "I feel like you're going into attack mode and disrespecting me. I'm not going to be part of that."
> "If you can't calm down, I will need to remove myself."
> "I'm having trouble calming down so I'm going to remove myself."
> "I want us to resolve this in a better way when we're both calmer."
> "I'll check back with you in an hour to see if we're both calm enough to talk."

Step # 3: Focus on your breathing.

When anger is on the rise, if you let your breathing become shallow and hurried, it can quickly escalate into full blown hyperventilation, a sure sign that you're not in control of yourself. This is certainly not a good time to try to have a productive conversation or reach resolution. After stepping away, your goal is to resume self-control. Find a quiet place to sit and focus on paying close attention to breathing deeply and slowly, taking in as much air as possible through your nose. When you exhale, blow your breath as far across the room as you can. Imagine all the stress, angry feelings, and toxins leaving your body. Continue focusing on slowing down until you feel calm and relaxed.

Step # 4: Scan your body to locate where your anger is getting stuck.

Because the mind-body-connection is strong, anger can literally surge into your muscles and organs, and change your oxygen level in seconds. Stress can surface as headache, stomach pain, soreness or tightening of the throat, chest pain, numbness in the hands, feet, or face, ringing in the ears, or even hearing or vision loss. Scan your body to find where physical signs of anger show up for you. Start at the top of your head and visualize relaxing each muscle, starting with your head, neck, shoulders, back, chest, abdominals, and upper and lower legs. Continue down your entire body, relaxing each part and every muscle group. Picture anger and stress draining out the bottom of your feet and moving away through the floor until it disappears. Then focus on letting go and relaxing the muscles and organs in the area with the greatest tension. Then repeat to yourself:

> "I am calm and relaxed."
> "I am calm and relaxed."
> "I am calm and relaxed."

Stretching and vigorous exercise can also help release toxic anger from your muscles. Continue the process of breathing and scanning your body until you are calm. Do not pass this step until you are in control of your anger and can devote energy to repair and solution-building.

Step # 5: Do something different.

After focusing on breathing and relaxing, if you are still having difficulty calming down, do something, anything, different to shift away from uncontrolled anger. Any action that interrupts your pattern, even if it's silly or unrelated to the situation, can help you get unstuck. Be as creative and discover the ways that are the most stress-relieving and pleasant to you. Here are a few suggestions:

> Go for a walk and continue practicing deep breathing and muscle relaxation.
> Get a drink of cold water.
> Meditate or pray on solutions.
> Take a soothing shower or bath.
> Do some vigorous exercise such as running, jumping jacks, swimming, or basketball.
> Do a calming exercise such as yoga or stretching.
> Sing or dance to your favorite music.
> Watch a funny movie or TV show.
> Share your feelings with a trusted friend and ask for advice and feedback.
> Pray, meditate, or visualize solutions to your current conflict.

Write down your thoughts and feelings, and continue writing until you've completely released your angry feelings.

Step # 6: Assess your self-management

Once you're under control, it's time to start building alternative responses. A simple guideline is to offer solutions that you're truly willing to try, and that you believe have a good chance of working. Remember, there is no right or wrong, only what will make a difference to the two of you. For some couples, listening is the key that makes the difference. For others it's conversation, and for still others separating and cooling off is the solution. Although you're in charge of designing your own alternate responses, here are seven general responses that work for many couples, and may also be useful to you:

Step # 1: Change defensiveness into responsiveness and open communication.

Once you are both calm, you can begin to lean into the issues and open up communication again, discuss what's gone wrong, and share your upset feelings with one another. Keep it short, say it once, then move on to searching for solutions together.

Try the1, 2, 3 rule of communication: three sentences only! In one sentence state:

> What you upset or bothered you in the situation
> How you feel about it
> What you want from your partner

Here are ways to begin each part of the process:

> "I'm really upset with you because I experienced…"
> "I am feeling angry, hurt, or sad because…"
> "I would appreciate…"

Step # 2: Just listen

Hold back from responding too quickly with defensiveness and attack. Simply listen closely to your partner's upset feelings, the feedback you're receiving, and what you're doing that your partner experiences as contributing to the problem. Your job is to take in the feedback without responding impulsively in anger. This will probably feel uncomfortable because it may be the opposite of your typical behavior, but it *is* critical to making this process work.

Step # 3: Acknowledge, apologize, and thank.

Acknowledge your partner's upset feelings and concerns to let them know you have listened. Ask if you have correctly understood what was said, and whether there is more that your partner needs to say. You might continue with:

> "I hear you saying…"
> "I am really sorry that I made you feel that way…"
> "Thank you for telling me I am doing that."
> "I will try my best to give you…"
> "Is there more you need to say?"

Step # 4: Offer your partner new possible solutions

Once you've listened, acknowledged, and thanked your partner, rather than staying stuck in problem-saturated talk, begin exploring possible solutions. Say:

"I will try my best to stop doing that, and I will do my best to do X …instead."

"What can I do to make this better for you?"

Step # 5: Check in

Make sure the solutions you are offering will make a difference to your partner. Remember to ask whether a suggested solution is what he/she is looking for. You might ask:

"Does this make a positive difference to you?"

"Is this what you are looking for?"

"Would this make you happy?"

Step # 6: Alternate and Repeat

Once you've had a chance to communicate and your partner has acknowledged and responded, reverse the process and allow your partner to express hurt feelings and needs. Commit to staying in the conversation until you achieve some resolution, even if it's to disagree. If you reach a deadlock and nothing new is being said, agree to finish the conversation and not bring up the issue again. You may need to respect your partner's right to say no to you or have a different opinion. Repeat this process until you have both expressed your feelings and be sure to avoid getting stuck in problem talk, complaining, and venting.

Step # 7: Deliver what you promised. Commit to only positive words and language.

Make sure you follow through and act on your promises to do something different. You may not be perfectly consistent at first, but make a solid effort to show your partner you are diligently trying to break your old habits and practice new ones. It is essential to remove angry, defensive language from your conversations. Stop retaliating and take responsibility for doing so. Whenever you feel you may be slipping back into old patterns, repeat these mantras: "Keep calm and respectful" and "Stay open, receiving, and giving."

Love Killer # 5 - Ordering, controlling, demanding

"You *should* do this! You *should* do that! You *should have* put that here! You *should* do it this way! You *should* do it *my* way! What is wrong with you, can't you do anything right?" Is your relationship infected with an awful case of the "should?" "Shoulding" can be triggered by any number of irritating behaviors. If your knee-jerk response to your partner is to become enraged begin ordering, commanding, and demanding, you are stuck in a power trip that may eventually take a serious emotional toll on your partner. If you are the partner on the receiving end of "shoulding," it's easy to lay all the blame on the one who is barking orders. But if you do nothing despite the "should," you're allowing yourself to be a victim and this destructive pattern to continue.

Berating, ordering, and demanding has no place in loving relationships. These are power grabs to gain control by being intrusive, withholding, or unresponsive. To use this strategy is shooting yourself in the foot, because a disrespectful, controlling style often results in the receiving partner being less motivated or willing to engage. My guideline is that adults do not have the right to tell each other what to do. Instead, make respectful requests.

Sparkling Point

No matter how much your partner annoys or upsets you, you have no right to order, command, or demand. Adult partners shouldn't tell each other what to do, they may request instead.

Striking a power balance in a relationship is like a finely performed dance. In ballroom dancing, it is an illusion that the man leads, and the woman simply follows. Great dance pairs move as one. The goal is to create the illusion of a smoothly gliding couple who are totally in sync. In order to do this, each partner must match the other's power, share the lead, and stay balanced. Ideally, a great couple shares power equally.

In healthy relationships power ebbs and flows, depending on the circumstances and necessary decisions that arise. One person seeking to retain all the power and control usually leads to considerable conflict and harms the intimate connection. The powerless partner may feel victimized, neglected, and even emotionally abused. Power and control should be balanced, fluid, and guided by standards of respect for one another. Think about your role in the imbalance of power. Do you act like a boss, parent, or teacher? Or, are you a passive victim who has allowed your partner to treat you like a naughty child? Both partners bear responsibility for part of the cycle and complement each other in a destructive way.

It's a mistake to buy into common myths that one person is to blame for an imbalance of power in a relationship, or that it's healthy for one partner to have authority and the other to have no voice. In our culture two common storylines about power problems in relationships exist. One version accuses women of being controlling, demanding nags who act like mothers and treat their husbands like naughty little boys. The other version insists that men are intimidating, selfish dictators who use money and physical intimidation to control women. There's actually some truth to both of these versions some of the time. What is missing in these narratives is that there is always a dance of power and control in relationships, no one acts alone, and each partner shares some of the responsibility.

Sparkling Point

Ordering, controlling, and demanding behaviors are authoritarian and dictatorial, not respectful or loving partnering.

For every partner who is too controlling, there is a partner on the receiving end who is too passive, allowing the behavior to happen.

Every couple must decide how to negotiate the inevitable dance of power and control. If you've been performing a destructive power dance for a long time, you may have already thrown up your hands in defeat and thought, "Why even bother to try to fix this. It's just the way it's always been with us, and there's no way out." But that doesn't have to be your truth. Every couple must decide how to negotiate the inevitable dance of power and control. Here are a few simple steps to rebalance power.

1. **Contain Your Impulses**

Limit your natural impulse to send or receive controlling, harsh communication. Whether you are the aggressive sender or the passive receiver, allowing ordering, commanding, and demanding communication is destructive. In other relationships you're probably capable of containing yourself, so why not approach your love relationship similarly?

How do you manage to keep your cool and stay respectful with friends, family, and co- workers? Perhaps you are motivated to keep it together because you don't want anyone to think poorly of you. The same standard of respect should be upheld in your love relationship as well. If you're on the receiving end, it's important to stop blaming your partner and look at your own role in the imbalance of power. Make sure you are consistently setting boundaries and letting your partner know you will no longer receive inappropriate ordering, commanding, or demanding.

2. **Stop playing the role of expert**

Giving expert advice or opinions can be condescending and usually results in partners shutting down. Do not lecture, give advice or offer opinions to your partner unless you are asked. Even then, offer it sparingly, choose your words wisely, and be prepared for your partner to reject what you say. To be heard, communicate in kind and respectful ways, even when you don't feel like doing it. You have a greater chance of reaching your partner by approaching the discussion with open communication that increases the chance of conversation, rather than giving directives and advice.

As a therapist, I stopped giving advice years ago when I realized that couples are more likely to improve when they create their own solutions to problems, rather than being told what to do by "the expert." As a teacher, I also know that lecturing is not the most effective way for anyone to learn. Especially for adults, the ability to listen to lecture rarely lasts more than a few minutes, and the ability to actually retain information is less.

3. Rebalance power

Stop blaming each other, and think about how you can equalize the power in your relationship. The more you let go of power, the more respect and love you will earn from your partner. Monitoring yourselves is important, and you should both initiate conversation and problem-solving when you feel your power balance is getting off track. Can you give away a portion of the power and control some of the time and share it when it's important to do so? Consider why you need to be in charge and what you may be getting out of trying to do so. You *do* have a perfect right to say what is bothering you and ask your partner to stop doing it.

4. Commit to only respectful statements

Compliments are a good way to begin a conversation with respect, and thank you is a good end. You might say:

> "I feel like you are trying to be in charge of me. Can you please not do that?"
> "I would appreciate if you ask me, not tell me."
> "You left me out of that decision, and I would appreciate being included."
> "I would really appreciate being part of this instead of staying silent and uninvolved."
> "When you don't tell me your opinion, I feel you don't care."
> "That's really bothering me. Can you please stop?"
> "Would you be so kind as to do this for me? I would really appreciate it"
> "I'm sorry I don't want to do that differently. It doesn't bother me as much as it bothers you."
> "I'm sorry that's bothering you, but it's not bothering me."

If your partner disagrees with you and continues to order, control and demand, set your boundary, step away, and do not participate until he/she can communicate in a respectful way.

5. Make space for partnering

If you've been the one in control for a long time, you may not want to admit it, but you may enjoy being in that role. Giving up power may not be easy. To have an equal partnership. You need to *be* an equal partner and open to making space for your partner to participate. It requires respect for differing opinions and decisions. Once you are both participating more equally, you will need to get comfortable accepting your partner's input, whether you agree with it or not. Your goal is not to create a relationship that is completely free of power struggles. In fact, that's impossible. The desire for control and power is a universal human need, and it's a given in the interactions between two people. The goal is to create equality with power that ebbs and flows. Will you become the ultimate power couple that willingly gives and takes power in a mutually shared dance?

Love killer # 6: Silent treatment

I would like you to try a short experiment with your partner. Each of you stand on either side of a wall. One of you may need to go outside to be on the other side of the wall, or go at least two rooms away from each other. Close the doors behind you and stay silent for a few minutes. Now try to communicate something important to your partner.

Obviously, you will not be able to see or touch each other, and most likely it will be difficult to hear one another beyond garbled sounds. Imagine remaining in this state for days, weeks, months, or even years. It would be almost impossible to resolve anything while you are walled off from each other. Do you think you would feel any connection or closeness if you stayed walled off like this for a long time? Yet, staying walled off from each other for long periods of time is exactly what many couples do. When they finally seek to get therapy, their connection and intimacy has totally disintegrated.

In times of conflict withdrawing into isolation is a destructive response. It is often experienced by partners as abandonment, disrespect, uncaring, and rageful. No good comes from this behavior. Issues may go dormant temporarily, but don't fool yourself into thinking you can "silent treatment" problems away. They simply go underground and fester. It may seem helpful to avoid conflict in the moment, but in the long run your chances of creating more explosive arguments will escalate. Withdrawing might avoid a confrontation in the moment, but unresolved feelings of anger or disappointment create emotional distance. If you continue to disconnect and isolate, building a wall, eventually the disconnect may become so great that you won't be able to hear, see, or touch each other emotionally, intellectually, or sexually.

Conflict is a given in all relationships, yet our culture views conflict as a negative experience rather than an opportunity for growth and compromise. If you're uncomfortable with conflict, you most likely learned that belief in your original family. If you grew up in a household where your parents frequently lashed out at one another with fighting, screaming, or getting physical, the message you got was that conflict is undesirable, frightening, or even dangerous. If your parents used silence and withdrawal to punish and control one another, you may be repeating that tactic to emotionally remove yourself from your partner in an attempt to keep power and control. Avoiding conflict by going radio silent and walling off is not a successful way to resolve differences.

Love Killer #6 – Silent Treatment

The silent treatment is usually a strategy learned in childhood to avoid unpleasant consequences such as being screamed at, punished harshly, or even hit. If you find it difficult to communicate during difficult moments with your partner, you may have observed arguments that seemed dangerous and scary. The only coping available to you might have been hiding, running away, suppressing your feelings, and being a good and silent child. Alternately, if you witnessed your parents being explosive and aggressive, lashing out and retaliating your communication style.

A helpful strategy to decrease silent treatment is to first change the way you *think* about conflict. You may believe conflict must be avoided at all costs because your earlier life experiences taught you that it is always dangerous. You can change your perceptions by focusing on new beliefs that are more empowering. A good starting point is to create phrases to shift your thinking and reinforce new ideas. Write down a few alternate productive phrases in a journal until you feel they are beginning to take hold and replace your old ways of thinking. Once new behaviors become an automatic part of your repertoire, you may not need to continue to recite the mantras or write in the journal, but make sure to keep your journal to refresh your memory in case the old beliefs and responses start to resurface. These mantras that may be helpful:

> Conflict is not dangerous or scary it's healthy and can bring us closer.
> My partner is not my mother, father, or sibling.
> I'm not a child, so I no longer need to act as if I hurting
> My partner is not trying to criticize, hurt,
> This is my adult partner whom I love and who loves me.
> My partner is simply feeling misunderstood right now.
> What does my partner need from me right now?
> How can we repair this misunderstanding?

Can you guess which three words are the most critical in healthy relationships? If you guessed "I love you!" you would be wrong. Those words are actually quite easy to speak. The words that have the most meaning to loving partners? They are: "Yes. I will." These three words are the most effective in keeping loving feelings strong and resolving conflicts quickly. It's important to complete that phrase to meet your partner's needs.

Communication that begins with the affirmative statement "*Yes, I will,* followed by proposed solutions, is an extremely inviting way to begin a conversation. I guarantee if you become an expert at saying "*yes, I will*", you *will* receive those other three magical words that everyone needs: "*I love you!*" Here are a few general suggestions you may find helpful:

"Yes, I will":
"Listen to you"
"Try to understand why you are upset"
"Try to understand your perspective on this topic"
"Stop doing what bothers you"
"Start doing more of what you ask for"

Sparkling Point

The remedy for silent treatment comes down to three words: "Simply,

Yes, I will…." AND whatever your partner wants, JUST DO IT!

Love killer # 7: Self – Centeredness

Technology has ushered in a new age of narcissism and self-centered entitlement. Many people have become consumed with gaining admiration while appearing perfect to the outside world. Seeking online recognition may be intoxicating, but the cost of an addiction to social media is high. As with all addictions, online and offline self-admiration and self-promotion can be very damaging to the health of a relationship. Now, in addition to the traditional worries about a partner's possible addictions to substances, gambling, or affairs, many people also worry about their partner's possible addictions to online pornography, virtual affairs, or obsessions with social media "friends" that may develop into affairs in real time. Many relationships are becoming casualties of this new narcissism and a partner's obsessive social media involvement.

Self-centeredness is placing focus on yourself and what you can *take*, not on what you can *give*. Drifting into a pattern of neglecting each other over many years usually results in disconnection that is beyond repair. When one partner begs for decades for and fails to receive affection, communication, time, and attention, their sense of self-esteem can be shattered. There is a limit to how much rejection a human being can tolerate. No response IS a response of malice and disrespect. If self-centeredness is left to fester, the partner on the receiving end eventually becomes totally emotionally depleted.

Narcissism is a fixation on oneself characterized by a person's obsession with his/her own life and an inability to give love, feel empathy, nurture, or validate another person. The concept of narcissism originated from the Greek myth of Narcissus, who was believed to be a handsome young man who was so self-centered and mesmerized by his own attractiveness that he fell in love with his reflection in a pool of water. Narcissus became so consumed with adoring his own image that he ignored the loving proclamations and advances of a beautiful mountain nymph named Echo. He spurned her love, ordered her to leave him alone, and spent his days obsessively admiring himself.

Narcissus eventually died of a broken heart once he realized his self-love would never fulfill him as much as the love of another.

Narcissus was not completely off base in his need to be admired, adored, and validated. What he craved was "mirroring" and "emotional holding", the normal human need to be validated by another. It's the fulfillment of that need that we all seek from birth that provides psychological security and promotes mental health and well-being. From the moment you are born, held, and capture the loving gaze of your primary caretakers, your attachment-seeking instinct kicks in. You realize that receiving love and being attached to another feels pretty darn good.

Mirroring is critically important in healthy loving relationships. Think of mirroring as your partner holding up a mirror to you and declaring how attractive, wonderful, and worthwhile you are. Emotional holding is the equivalent of surrounding your partner with an embrace of love and caring. If your partner is not providing you with mirroring and emotional holding, you may be stuck in an unhealthy relationship with a narcissistic partner. Mirroring is the way a partner reflects your own lovable and valuable attributes back to you. Emotional holding is providing a nurturing, safe, emotional environment in which listening, support, guidance, and love is consistently guaranteed to your partner.

Your partner shouldn't have to keep asking for what they want and need. Years of self-centeredness and narcissism on the part of one partner takes a tremendous toll on the other. The consequences can be major depression, anxiety, emotional exhaustion, numbness, or uncontrolled rage. How much time are you spending online, promoting yourself and building relationships with virtual friends? How often are you really connecting and giving love, time, and energy to your partner?

Ask yourself, where do your partner's needs fit into your list of priorities? Are they at the top or the bottom, or not on the list at all? If you're not into technology or social media, are there other priorities that are on the top of your list? Is most of your free time consumed with your career, working out, hanging out with friends, golf, tennis, or shopping? If you answered the questions above honestly and realized that virtually everything else in your life is a priority except your partner, there's a good chance your relationship will not survive. If you are focused only on your own needs being met, and have neglected your partner's needs, eventually your emotional, physical, and sexual intimacy *will* die.

You can rationalize away isolation and neglect in your relationship, but if your partner is not empathic, lacks the ability to give, and does not put you first, you may eventually feel so emotionally depleted that you will have no feelings left. If you accept being neglected over a long period of time, you may eventually pay a serious price in depression, anxiety, or physical illness. You may even end up just like Narcissus: loveless, empty, and emotionally dead. The antidote for self-centeredness is shifting to selflessness to create a more loving, giving balance in your relationship.

Here is a five-step pattern for creating a gold standard of selflessness.

Step # 1: Focus on what you can give, not what you can get.

If you are the receiver of your partner's neglect. Quarantine yourself from your partner's self-centeredness, and refuse to accept that behavior as "good enough". You deserve to be an object of love and desire, not a neglected convenience.

Step # 2: Change your focus

Get the center of attention off yourself, minimize self-*centeredness* and maximize self*lessness*. Reverse the lens of admiration and focus in the opposite direction on your partner. Selflessness is the ability to keep one's own needs in check, place another's needs and wishes above your own, give empathy, and "mirror" admiration and adoration onto another. If your partner is depressed or anxious and complains of feeling empty and lonely, look within and ask yourself what part you are playing.

Step #3: Tune in to your partner's deepest desires and provide them.

Do you really know what makes your partner feel loved and admired? It's incredibly important to tune in closely to your partner's needs and discover exactly what she/he wants. If you neglect to tune in, you can create as much damage as doing nothing at all. The message you are transmitting is that you don't really care or remember what your partner needs from you. You're also saying that you are not willing to be responsible for delivering in this partnership. Commit to checking in a few minutes each day with your partner about how close you are coming to meeting their needs. Tuning in is important to know what actions make a difference to your partner. Don't assume you know what your partner wants. Tune in by directing your energy, focus, and actions towards your partner's desires, and follow through on what you promise to give.

Step # 4: Give five gifts a day

Relationship happiness is directly related to small, daily habits of consistent giving through loving actions. In fact, small, thoughtful gestures matter more than elaborate date nights, weekend trips, expensive gifts, or sexual marathons. The latter are great, but less important than mirroring, validating, and holding your partner in high regard.

Gifts are random acts of kindness and affection that validate and keep loving feelings alive. An added benefit is decreased anger and conflict. Stop and think about how much time it actually takes to hug and kiss, send a text, leave a message, or send an email. I'm certain you'll find those actions can be completed in seconds. Isn't your partner worth that amount of your time?

Five gifts a day is a reasonable expectation. They can be as small as a random snuggle, a cup of coffee made exactly right, making two breakfasts instead of one, a quick text during the day saying "thinking of you, hope you are having a good day", hugs and kisses upon arriving home, or sharing evening chores. These are the type of loving actions that let your partner know you are keeping them front and center in your thoughts. One action first thing in the morning, during the day, when you arrive home, and in the evening and you've got four already! Committing to five small gifts of loving kindness each day reinforces the idea for your partner that you still care.

Step # 5: Use technology to connect, not disconnect

While addiction to social media can isolate you from your partner, it can also be used to strengthen your connection. Are you willing to give your partner equal time? Can you spare thirty seconds to stay in contact? If you make an effort five times a day, that amounts to 2 ½ minutes. No more excuses! Don't let technology become a barrier between and your partner. Use it to stay connected and maximize your closeness.

Step # 6: Maximize your holding time

Stop placing your partner on hold, literally and emotionally, and increase your listening, support, and caring. Don't make your partner beg for your response or emotional support. Minimize neglect and make time to hold your partner in the loving arms of your responsiveness, concern, and caring. Make sure you are providing dedicated holding time for your partner. That doesn't simply mean physical holding, it also means holding them emotionally as your highest priority. In the same way you learned to create a positive feedback loop of communication, create a positive feedback loop of love, caring, and validation.

Be the partner you want

You have a choice to make about the type of partner you want to be. Will you continue to be like Narcissus, focusing on your own self-admiration and adoration? Or will you choose to get over yourself, maintain a reasonable balance, shut down excessive technology, and start giving your partner your full attention? If you shift your focus from what you can get to what you can give, you will create a positive emotional feedback - loop, and receive more of the love, affection, and caring you want.

If you are the partner on the receiving end of self - centeredness, will you choose to protect yourself from neglect? If you have a self-centered partner, you are giving him/her permission to continue to neglect you by sending the message that it is acceptable to neglect, ignore, and mistreat you that way. Disrespect, defensiveness, uncontrolled anger, passive aggressive retaliation, ordering, controlling, and demanding, silent treatment, and self- centeredness will eat away at the health of your relationship unless you take action. A word to the wise: a fire that is not consistently fueled eventually burns out. If you fuel the fire of your loving relationship and give it your all, you will receive more love and fulfillment than you could ever have possibly imagined.

❖ PLAY # 15

Spinning Straw into Gold Standards

Rather than examining the details of your problems, it will serve you better to shift your energy into building solutions as quickly as possible. Your next step is to decrease destructive behaviors and create new gold standards. This play is intended to be an overview for you to assess which of the seven love killer behaviors need improvement, contemplate the behaviors, and focus on what you want your standards to be for each. Remember that you are unique, and as a couple, you are the experts who know where your most critical needs for change are.

Draft a list of proposed gold standards to share and negotiate with your partner. Focus on what you want more of, and what each of you can each start doing right now to make a difference. Be as specific as possible. Use the questions below as a guideline for beginning your new contract. For each of the seven love killer behaviors contemplate the following:

What areas are going well for us at this time?

What areas were going well for you in the beginning of your relationship?

What is your detailed vision of what new standards will look like?

Gold Standards Proposal List

Email your Gold Standard proposals to each other. Then, set aside time to discuss and agree on a joint contract that is comfortable for both of you.

Play # 15

Takeaway Notes

❖ PLAY #16

Redefining Respect

Complete the following on your own:

How do I define respect in my relationship? State specific actions and words you consider to be most respectful.

What do I believe my partner considers respectful behavior?

What boundaries do I want to set for myself? What disrespectful behaviors am I no longer willing to accept?

What is going well between us that I consider respectful and productive?

Specifically, who is doing what at those times?

If you are having difficulty identifying current respectful behaviors, search for them in your past. If you fail to find respectful behaviors in the past, use the miracle visualization to imagine how the two of you will be behaving respectfully in your future.

Make time to discuss respect and disrespect in your relationship. Protect your privacy and give each other your full attention by turning off all technology, including your television, and do not allow interruptions, even from your children. Share your thoughts with each other about the exercises above. Listen attentively and do not interrupt each other. After each one of the four parts, acknowledge what you heard your partner speak. Then make an agreement to actions you are promising to deliver. Here are a few guidelines for your conversation:

"I will commit to…"

"Does that make a difference to you?"

"Is there anything else you want me to understand or do?

Make a "cooling off" plan by stating what steps you will both take when you are at risk of deteriorating into disrespect.

Play # 16

Takeaway Notes

❖ PLAY # 17

Slaying the Deadly Triad

Take a moment to think about how your anger surfaces and where it gets stuck in your body:

List all possible ways you can calm yourself when you begin to experience anger. Let your ideas flow freely and do not edit yourself.

Make a list of all possible alternative responses to negotiate anger, differences, and conflict in a constructive manner.

Check in with your partner to discuss your list of responses to the question above. Ask your partner which of the above would be most helpful. If some or none are not helpful, ask your partner what would be preferable?

Play # 17

Takeaway Notes

❖ PLAY # 18

Assessing Your Power Balance

Consider the role you play in your relationship's power imbalance. Are you an aggressive partner who orders, commands, and demands, or are you a silent, passive recipient/victim? If you are the aggressor, ask:

What is my need to order, command, or demand of my partner, and what benefit do I gain from behaving in that way?

Am I willing to do whatever it takes to control of my behavior?

If you are the passive receiver, ask what stops you from stepping up as an equal partner?

What would it take to break my part in this pattern?

Whether you are the giver or the receiver, list the things you say and do that contribute to the imbalance of power:

Now write down an antidote for each change to which you will commit to rebalance and equalize the power in your relationship:

Have discussion of the changes on which you have agreed and start building solutions with your partner. Be careful not to return to venting, complaining, or problem talk.

Take turns say:

"From this point on I will do my best to keep our relationship balanced by..."

Stopping:

Starting:

Ask your partner if these steps would be helpful.

If the answer is "yes", that's terrific, and end your discussion there. If the answer is "no" ask what would be more helpful.

Play # 18

Takeaway Notes

❖ **PLAY # 19**

Just Say Yes!

Answer the following:

What does my partner ask for and want the most from me?

On a scale of 1-100 what percentage of the time do I say *yes* to my partner?

Based on what you think makes a difference to your partner, list ten ways you can complete the phrase "Yes", I will…

1.

2.

3.

4.

5.

6.

7.

8.

9.

10.

Think about how conflict and upset feelings were handled in your family when you were

a child. Write down your top three beliefs about conflict:

Now change those statements and beliefs by creating three new statements you can use as self-talk mantras.

Now together, share your ten ways to say YES!

Ask your partner to choose the three most helpful and meaningful ways to say YES!

Keep the list for future reference.

Play # 19

Takeaway Notes

❖ **PLAY # 20**

Sneaky Surprises

Ask your partner to provide you with a list of small experiences they would enjoy on a daily basis. Make a list of ten small actions you believe will make your partner feel happy and loved.

For one week, be sneaky and secretly surprise your partner a minimum of five small, loving actions every day. Do not discuss until the end of the week. On a scale of 1-10, ask your partner how happy they felt about your relationship last week? Specifically, what happened that made them feel happy and cared for?

What happened in the past week they would like you to repeat?

More:

The Same:

Less:

CHAPTER 5

Sparkling Points Summary

It's not familiarity or an extended length of time that depletes relationships. Sparkle fades when couples lower their standards and expectations and replace them with destructive, unloving habits. No matter how long you and your partner have been stuck in dysfunction, there is hope that you can improve your standards and boost them to gold!

A deadly love killer is any action or lack of action that your partner experiences as upsetting, hurtful, disrespectful, or unloving.

Disrespect is the #1 killer of loving feelings. Without mutual respect, civility is compromised. Disrespect includes any harsh, unkind, or demeaning verbal or non-verbal actions.

If your partner invades your emotional and physical boundaries and lets disrespect run rampant, you put your relationship at risk. Over time it *will* chip away at respect, trust, and closeness

You are in charge of how your partner treats you. Each time you do nothing in response and accept disrespect, you give your partner permission to continue to treat you that way.

Once you clearly define respect and disrespect, pay attention to your partner's definitions, and commit to staying within those guidelines.

You can guarantee respect by

committing to a gold standard of respecting yourself and receiving and giving only respectful interactions in your relationship.

Defensiveness is any action used to avoid accepting responsibility for your behavior and receiving feedback from your partner about how she/he experiences you.

Defensiveness extends conflict and gets you less of what you want.

It's a guaranteed lose-lose strategy that solves nothing and creates distance and misunderstanding.

Lashing out with any form of uncontrolled anger and attacking your partner is emotional abuse. It harms everyone: the giver, the receiver, and children who are the observers.

No matter how much your partner annoys or upsets you, you have no right to order, command, or make demands of them. Adult partners may make requests of each other, but should not tell each other what to do.

Ordering, controlling, and demanding behaviors are authoritarian, dictatorial, and disrespectful. For every partner who is too controlling, there is a partner on the receiving end who is too passive and allows it to happen.

The remedy for silent treatment and isolating comes down to three words: "Yes, I will…." AND, whatever your partner wants, JUST DO IT!

CHAPTER 6

Igniting Your Erotic

Words of Wisdom

"You should be kissed and often, and from someone who knows how."

- Rhett Butler, Character in *Gone with the Wind*

"To men sex is an emergency, and no matter what we're doing, we can to be ready in two minutes. Women, on the other hand are like a fire. They are very exciting, but the conditions have to be exactly right for it to occur."

- Jerry Seinfeld, comedian

"Eroticism is not sex per se, but the qualities of vitality, curiosity, and spontaneity that make us feel alive. The erotic is an antidote to death"

- Esther Perel, author of *Mating in Captivity*

"We've been conditioned by our culture and a myriad of relationship gurus to regard passion as more of a passing sensation rather than a durable force. We are told that the sexual fires that burned so brightly at the start of love inevitably burn down."

- Dr. Sue Johnson, author of Hold Me Tight

From wild passion to sex - starved

Has your once passionate sex life transformed into a sex-starved relationship? Does sexuality after a certain age really matter anyway? After a couple is together a long time, isn't it easier to simply accept sexless companionship as the norm? But is it inevitable that erotic passion and vibrant sex will die after the first stage of falling in love? If that flame has burned out you may feel those feelings can never be reignited.

Sexless relationships are not uncommon today because as a society, we have bought into negative narratives about sexuality. These storylines are not truths, however, they are simply myths that have grown popular over time. You can choose to believe them, do nothing, and settle for a life without passion. If you do so, you might be lucky enough to be among the forty percent of couples who make it. Nonetheless, accepting a life without sexual intimacy is far more likely to put you at risk for being among the sixty percent of couples who don't make it. Your relationship may survive, but just barely, and there certainly is a difference between surviving and thriving. I often hear couples in therapy rationalize negative beliefs about sexuality in the following ways:

We have no time for sex- we are too busy and too tired.

Too many other things are a priority.

We've both aged and changed physically and sex is embarrassing.

We don't sleep together anymore so it's not possible to have sex.

Too many things bother us, he snores, she's hot or cold.

Sex just isn't important anymore.

I don't believe any of the above are valid reasons not to have a fulfilling, passionate sex life. Debunking common myths can help you to begin to move forward into more positive stories about sexuality. Here are some suggested shifts:

Your sexual connection is just as important as every other aspect of your life.

Everyone has some time in their week when they are not tired and sex is possible.

You can commit to working as a team to making intimacy a priority.

Physical changes are a normal part of aging and should be gracefully embraced.

You don't need to sleep in the same bed to have an active sex life.

There are many solutions for physical problems such as snoring and hot flashes.

Sparkling Point

If you stop putting energy into your sex life, the flames of passion will burn out.

What many people don't realize is that consistent sexual rejection and neglect of a partner can cause tremendous emotional harm. Lack of intimacy can erode a person's self–esteem, and create intense feelings of abandonment, loneliness, and depression. The emotional, intellectual, and spiritual parts of the relationship will suffer as well. Often, couples that have ignored each other's needs for years become detached and numb to one another.

In therapy sessions, know a couple has given up when I see neglected appearances, poor hygiene, extreme discomfort sitting near one another, refusal to hold hands, hug, or touch. Although the details of each couple's story may differ, the theme is usually the same: they've settled for a sex-starved relationship. I've heard many sad stories from couples who truly love one another but have lost their intimate connection. They've gotten bored or have let too much anger and resentment build.

I once had a husband in session say: "We don't bother to have sex anymore because it just doesn't work and it seems like it would just be too much work to fix it. I initiate it a few times a year just because I feel obligated, but I wouldn't say it's anything I enjoy or that gives me any pleasure. Sex has become a cold, physical thing. We're not connected anymore. We don't say good morning, hello, or goodbye, let alone hug or kiss. It doesn't matter how I invite her, what I do or say, what I wear, or how I look. Nothing seems to turn her on anymore. I think we had sex last Christmas and it's almost Christmas again, so maybe we'll get lucky. I've never been the affectionate type and I'm not into holding hands or any of those little things. I just can't give that to her."

His wife responded with: "My husband avoids me all week long. He literally hides in the bathroom before the kids and I leave in the morning so he doesn't have to help or deal with us, nor does he connect with me in anyway during the day. I feel like he's a boarder that comes and goes and does his own thing. There's no affection or warmth anymore, yet would you believe he still demands that we schedule sex twice a week so he can get his selfish needs met?"

Another husband reported, "She deprives me of the one thing I want the most, sexual connection. It's like the more I want that, the more she withholds it. I think it's a power play to be in control, and it's cruel. I feel like that part of me has died little by little over the years. They say one tiny cut won't kill you, but a thousand tiny cuts will. Death by a thousand cuts, that's what's I feel in this relationship."

Another wife said, "It feels like all the sexuality has been sucked out of our relationship. We just exist and everything else comes first: kids, house, groceries, laundry, and work. We don't spend any quality time together, let alone have sex, which that isn't even a thought anymore. We don't hug, kiss, or cuddle. We're just too exhausted and disinterested."

Are these stories simply the inevitable outcome of the slow death of passion over time? It is true that as a relationship progresses over years, familiarity and aging kick in, and sexuality changes. Women experience various hormonal changes in their childbearing, peri-menopausal, menopausal, and post-menopause years. Men also experience physical and hormonal changes that affect sexual interests, drive, and stamina. In the normal course of life, a person's ability to turn on and respond to touch may change. Also, some prescription medications may have an impact on desire. But despite normal developments, your intimacy *can* be recovered as long as you are willing to modify your expectations of great sex, make adaptations, and create a new style and standard of sexuality.

Sparkling Point

Despite the challenges of long-term relationships and aging, you shouldn't settle for a life without affection and passionate sex. Doing so can harm your physical, emotional, intellectual, and spiritual well-being, as well as put you at risk for outside temptations to fill that void.

The benefits of keeping your erotic energy alive are many. Long-term fulfilling sex creates acceptance, high self-esteem, secure bonding, and better physical and mental health. Great sex also creates deeper emotional attachment and lessens anger and conflict. The reverse is also true: greater emotional intimacy, togetherness, and less anger sets the stage for fulfilling lovemaking. Mutual giving of affection and initiation of sex are important at every age because it provides validation for your partner and sends the message that they are still loved, wanted, and accepted.

Sparkling Point

You don't have to settle for a mediocre or non-existent sex life. There is another option: re-ignite and evolve your erotic energy! If you don't keep feeding that fire, it will eventually burn out.

Many couples tell me they simply don't know where to begin to get their sexual connection back. What follows next are specific steps for reawakening your passion, which begin with warming up the embers of emotional connection through fun, friendship, and companionship.

Sparkling Point

It is a mistake to try to re-ignite sexual intimacy without first warming up your emotional connection through fun, friendship, and companionship.

These elements are critically important to maintaining vibrant intimacy because they create a positive feedback loop of emotional closeness that fuels affection and desire. Take a moment to consider your desire for sex when there's emotional distance, hostility, and conflict. Do you really feel like being intimate with your partner when you're having no fun or not feeling close? You might assume that most men would answer that it makes no difference, and they would still want sex anyway, and there is some truth to that! Yet, in therapy many men report they don't want sex with a partner who is disinterested, because that becomes boring and unfulfilling. Many women say they have become disinterested in sex because they no longer feel emotional warmth, affection, or respect. Women tend to need consistent emotional connection to open up sexually.

There is no reason why desire and connection should decrease over time. When you first met, there may have been magnetic physical attraction and a high degree of lust. Passion may have initially been ignited through small expressions of affection and cuddling. But you need much more than that to keep sexuality vibrant for the long term. Most new couples make a great effort to invest not only in their sexual connection, but create fun, friendship, and companionship. Intimacy is also created by discussing important topics such as life dreams, goals, beliefs, and philosophies. When I ask couples what first attracted them besides looks and lust, they often relate that their partner showed interest, was a good listener, opened up, shared joys, worries, and values. You can call upon the memories of those interactions and bring them forward to reactivate fun and friendship.

Sparkling Point

The triple threat-secret great couples know, friendship, and companionship fuel erotic passion.

If fun, friendship, and companionship fade, you lose the glue of togetherness that is the foundation of affection and great sex. When a couple first begins therapy, I ask them to rate their relationship for fun, friendship, and companionship on a scale of 1-10. This question measures overall relationship satisfaction. When the response is a "deer in headlights" moment, and a couple cannot remember the last time they had fun, hugged, kissed, or had sex, I know they are in real trouble. They are often exhausted, demoralized, and well on their way to considering a break up.

One wife replied to the scaling question with: "Oh my God, *zero!* The *last* thing I want is being near him, let alone having *sex* with him! The way he ignores me, calls me names, and mocks me has taken a toll. I don't feel any connection to him anymore. We used to be best friends and talk about everything, but at this point, I don't feel like we're even acquaintances. I'm barely hanging on by a thread, just getting through each day because the kids are still at home, but it's a real chore."

Her husband replied, "*She's* the one that's no fun. We don't enjoy doing anything together anymore. She's turned cold to sex and I can't take the constant rejection. It's just easier for me to block out that part. We're way past the stage of going on dates, and hot sex was out the window ages ago. We haven't slept in the same bed for ten years, so how could we be having sex? I'm just here because it's convenient, it makes sense financially, and frankly the idea of starting over seems like too much work."

I asked another husband if he knew what his wife considered fun. After staring blankly for some time, he offered, "The monster truck show or the shooting range?"

"That's all you got?" I asked. He responded: "That's all I got! We do everything by ourselves because I hate everything she likes, and she hates everything I like. She's a beach person and I like hiking in the mountains. She likes concerts and I can't stand them. I like motorcycle riding and she will have nothing to do with it. Last year we had a huge argument because she wanted to go to Europe, and I told her I had no interest because there was nothing to do there. And, our sex life is totally in the dumpster."

The sad part of this story is that this couple previously had a great deal of fun and enjoyed adventurous day trips, musical concerts, sports events, and a fulfilling sex life.

Another couple had this interchange, "I can't take you anymore," the husband snarled.

"You always throw a wet blanket on any fun we're having. I have more fun when you stay home. Now the day is ruined, and I'm sure sex is out of the question *as usual!*"

"You're so selfish, and it's all about you!" replied his wife. "Sex is the only thing you really care about. Why would I want to have sex with you after all that screaming? You have no respect for me!"

"It's all your fault we don't have sex!" he replied. "Your screaming is sex repellant!" It was sad for me to hear that this couple wasn't able to enjoy being in the moment. Not only had they lost their connection to fun and friendship, their sex life and emotional intimacy was suffering as well. Do the stories of these couples resonate with you?

Sparkling Point

Problems with your erotic life may seem hopeless, but they are not necessarily serious. There are simple ways to re-ignite erotic energy and jumpstart your fun, friendship, and companionship.

Have you considered that your problems may have simple solutions and may even be funny? Very few problems are true tragedies, so why hold onto the belief that yours are too serious to solve, when you could use the option of humor? If you've become too problem-focused about your sexuality, try shifting your focus by planning fun experiences that will increase pleasure and bring back desire. You may be thinking, oh my God, now we have to *plan* fun? *Yes,* you may have to plan fun until it once becomes natural.

Skip the cliches of date nights, movies, or sunset walks on the beach. Those experiences are fine, but they don't require much imagination and can become boring and repetitive. Let your creative juices flow and don't be afraid to step it up and plan outrageous fun that will bring back your joy. Why not try something the two of you have never done before?

How about recreating some of the fun and adventures you had when you first got together? Make sure you know what your partner considers fun, rather than planning activities only *you* think are fun. If you don't like the same things, take turns and alternate the planning. Try to enjoy each other's interests, even if you don't feel like it. Here are five tips to re re-energize your fun, friendship, and companionship:

1. **Re-awaken your childhood joys.**

Get back in touch with your childhood lack of inhibition to make fun from simple, every day experiences. Reactivate those now and let the laughter begin! Take a moment to consider why children are often able to create fun for hours on end in almost every situation. They chase snowflakes, jump waves at the beach, hide in cardboard boxes, make forts out of blankets, and simply play in dirt. Children use whatever is available to them in the moment. Your childhood may hold the keys to creating ways you can feel oy in the present. What gave you the most laughter in childhood? Did you spend happy ours biking, dancing, singing, making crafts, playing your favorite sport, or creatively making up fun things to do? Did your family enjoy picnics, carnivals, or amusement parks?

2. **Start fun now instead of postponing it.**

Perhaps you dream about indulging in new activities such as driving cross country, practicing yoga, or playing pickleball. Don't save these activities for your future! Create a "Live in The Present" list! If you don't have a list, get on it, time's a wasting!

3. **Stay in the moment.**

Center yourself and settle into simply being in the present and enjoying every opportunity to find joy, silliness, and laughter in everyday situations. You may be missing chances for fun because you're too serious, focused on the past, or too worried about the future. Stop ruminating about mistakes you've made or what your future may hold. Focus on the joy you can have now in the present moment.

4. Dismiss fear

Are you concerned about what others will think or telling yourself you simply don't have as much energy as you once did? Push yourself past fear and embarrassment and really let yourself go! Keep your focus off thoughts that may hold you back, such as: "I'm too old, it's too late, family and friends will think we're crazy, or fun isn't important at this stage of life." Focus on the best-case scenario of trying something new, and see what happens!

5. Recharge your friendship energy.

If you're skeptical about re-establishing friendship and can't remember what initially glued the two of you together, you can still create close friendship, even if you never had it. Think of how you make and keep friendships in other areas of your life. Those skills easily transfer to your primary partnership.

Sparkling Point

No matter how disconnected your relationship has become, if you started out as great friends and companions, you can re-create that togetherness.

1. Use other long friendships as role models for your love relationship

Do you have friendships that have lasted decades? What has enabled them to thrive? Friendships that stand the test of time are usually involve consistent support, respect, non-judgment, and good listening. On the other hand, consider if you have remained friends with anyone who is unsupportive, critical, self-involved, or insensitive to your needs. What style friend are you to your partner? Do you treat your partner as well as you do long-term friends? An abiding friendship requires consistent giving and support. Your expectations of friendship in other parts of your life can be a guideline to set the standard for friendship in your love relationship.

2. Send your partner small daily reminders to show you are thinking of them. If your partner does the same, make sure you acknowledge and reciprocate.

Maintaining strong friendship in your love relationship isn't simply about spending time together. Instead of staying passive and isolating, commit to being proactive and consistently invite each other into friendship every day, even just a bit. A sure way to turn off your partner is to reject their efforts at friendship, so make sure you accept and reciprocate. Technology has made it easy to stay connected; these days it literally takes seconds to send a text or email. There are even bracelets that each partner can light up during the day to send a message of love. There are still the classic ways of connecting: a quick phone call, sharing a cup of coffee or lunch, or the old standby, quickie sex.

3. **Validate and compliment your partner.**

Give your partner the same validation, mirroring, and emotional holding you give to your best friends. Find ways to "like" your partner and send the message, "I've always liked you, I still like you, and I will continue to like you." We have become so addicted to accumulating social media friends and followers, "likes" and "hearts" that real connections have gotten lost. We all crave connection and validation from our significant other. Think about the warm feelings that may be created if you put as much energy into showing you like your partner in real time as much as you do your online friends. Little moments of recognition show your partner you still care.

4. **Have your partner's back 24/7.**

A great partner is one who doesn't put their partner on hold, ever! Be there 24/7 for your partner and make that your first priority, no matter what. Give constructive support, tune in, listen, and stay connected with patience. When asked to listen, make sure you ask your partner if they want only listening, support, advice, or opinion. Allow your partner's needs to become your needs.

Now that you have guidelines for re-energizing your fun, friendship, and companionship, you're ready to start to reawaken your passion. Your vision of your erotic life together can be whatever you desire. There is no right or wrong, correct or incorrect, true or false. Every couple is unique, and every stage of sexuality is specific to each of you. I encourage you to take a broad view of sexuality, not to focus on intercourse as the only route to achieving pleasure. As sex researcher Dr. Emily Nagoski advises, keep pleasure as the first priority and desire will naturally follow.

Guidelines for re-igniting your erotic

1. **Open communication is critical**

Great communication is the key to great sex, period. It's important to continue to communicate about intimacy as you age. Your likes, dislikes, and needs may change, and it is important to keep checking in with one another on how it's going. Because your sexual needs may change over time, consistently communicate new information about your desires, what is going, and what needs improvement. It's not only important to communicate *during* sex, conversations are also necessary outside of the bedroom.

Remember to create a positive feedback loop by saying, "Yes, I will". Also remember to lighten up, have fun, and laugh! Sex should be light, refreshing, rejuvenating, and draw you closer. Remember: sex is FOR PLAY!

When discussing your sex life, there's nothing to be gained from criticism or negativity. Use only compliments and solution-building conversations. Be careful not to infect your sex life with negative complaints. If you have a concern, communicate using the same one, two, three rule of communication previously suggested for other areas of your relationship. Compliments are a great way to open up communication, because it's human nature to be more open to a suggestion when it's prefaced with something positive about yourself. Begin with the conversation with statements such as: "You're really terrific at…", "I love when you…" "It's perfect when you …", "I love our intimate life because…".

Another tip is to use the word *and* instead of the word *but*. *But* usually creates a negative message that most people tune out. When a sentence begins with "but", most people assume: "here comes the part where I'm going to be criticized." Starting with a compliment and saying *and* instead is a good way to lead into suggestions to create a positive communication feedback loop, and prevent defensiveness and attacking. After giving compliments, use the one, two, three technique of communication and offer one sentence about each of the following: What you are upset or concerned about, how do you feel about it, and what you want. Receive feedback and respond by thanking your partner for what has been shared. Acknowledge your partner's needs and offer solutions. Monitor your sexual closeness and make sure you communicate when you feel you're getting too isolated from one another.

2. Banish the seven love– killer behaviors

If you protect your relationship from the seven love-killers, there's a good chance your intimate life will stay vibrant with little effort. Dealing with conflict productively, keeping communication open, and focusing on giving usually leads to loving feelings that create more desire. Do you really want to be physically close or have sex with a partner who is neglectful?

3. Stage your sanctuary

Does your bedroom have its own erotic sparkle or is it messy or sorely in need of a refreshing? It should be your private retreat for more than just sex, a place to recharge in ways you both enjoy activities such as watching TV, snuggling, napping, or catching up on the day with pillow talk. Your bedroom should reflect your sexual style as a couple and be pleasing, comfortable, and inviting. Is it a catch-all for clothes, work papers, storage boxes, laundry, and a hangout for your kids and pets? Your redesign might include luxurious linens, fresh flowers, candles, enticing colognes and oils, your favorite movie, music, a mini-fridge, or whatever turns on both of you. Or, you might love hanging out under the covers for a football game, pizza, and beer. A TV in the bedroom is okay as long as it doesn't get in the way of your private couple time. I recall one couple who had managed to figure out how to watch TV or read and have sex at the same time! Their strategy was funny and brilliant, and it stemmed from their open communication and ability to play.

One more critical accessory: a lock for your door and a "do not disturb, no kids or pets allowed" sign. If your bedroom is a place where kids and pets can barge in at any moment, you're not maintaining protective boundaries. This doesn't mean that you can't enjoy special moments with the whole family piled into your bed for a movie and popcorn. But if that's a daily occurrence, you're sending your partner the message that your private couple time is not a priority.

Remember that your kids learn how to be intimate by observing you. It's good for children to observe your desire for privacy and affection, and also to learn to delay their own gratification. They *will* survive if they are not the center of your universe for an hour or two. Of course, you value your children and want to be there for them whenever they need you, but it's also important to make private couple time a priority. Certainly, there needs to be a strong boundary around your sex life, and your children should not be privy to it, but it is healthy for older children to know that you have a positive relationship with sex and it's an important part of loving. Remember that how your children see you interact with one other is the blueprint for their adult relationships. Do you want their future relationships to be cold and unaffectionate, or warm and loving?

4. Style each other

Have you had a sex style makeover with your partner recently? Become you own stylists by checking in on what turns on your partner the most, then get going on that makeover! If you don't already know your partner's favorite attire, turn-ons, and foreplay moves, check in and find out! Keeping up your appearance, cleanliness, and health, is not only good for your own physical and emotional well-being, it also lets your partner know you still care about attracting and pleasing them.

Women tend to get turned on by romance and emotional connection throughout the day. Some prefer their partner in a suit, shirt and tie, and cologne. Others may prefer the scruffy, sweaty, baseball cap, "just worked out" look. Men tend to be much more visual, and some have very specific tastes in sexy lingerie. Others love seeing their partner in casual sweats, their shirt, messy hair and glasses, or the surprise of nothing underneath. If your partner likes freshly brushed teeth and a freshly showered body, pay attention to those details and make sure you do those things. If you know your partner likes a fit body, keep that in mind as well. Once you tune in to the appearance your partner likes the most, deliver!

5. Go on an erotic shopping spree

No matter your age or stage of life, accessories and toys can refuel your erotic energy in a hurry. An erotic shopping spree can be a huge turn on, or at the very least, a hilarious adventure! You don't need to buy anything as wild as a leather poodle mask or fifty shades of chains and cuffs if that's not your style. If you're too shy for an erotic shop or such a place is too raunchy for you, choose an elegant, small lingerie shop where you can find classy lingerie, cute toys, and female friendly videos. Yes, there are videos with interesting plots that women find appealing! If you're too embarrassed to go to a local shop, a day trip out of town can be fun. Sexual aids and toys are also easily accessible, sold in large chain pharmacy stores which have entire sections for intimacy aids and toys. You can even find them in the travel size section! Surprising your partner by shopping for your favorite aphrodisiacs online together can also be a great fun.

6. **Do one small thing different each time**

If you've gotten stuck in repetitive, boring sex, using the same old automatic moves for years, try doing one small thing different each time. Imagining a new variety of moves can snowball and create exciting improvements. Even small differences can be transformative, and experimentation can be funny and challenging! Stay open to all ideas, and remember it's important to respect one another's boundaries. Be sure to be respectful of what your partner is willing to try, and also *not* willing to try. Open communication is the key, as well as keeping criticism and negativity out of the conversation. Say: "Yes, I like that, do more of that" or "That one, not so much!" Just like visiting the eye doctor!

7. **Shrink wrap hugs, twenty/six hugs and kisses**

Couples who have let their sex life deteriorate sometimes tell me they feel emotionally cold, have no desire left, and are paralyzed about how to start to get comfortable with sex again. If you haven't been with each other in a long time, a good technique to warm up is what I call a "shrink wrap hug." Wrap your bodies tightly around each other and get into the tightest hug possible. Try to pace with each other by breathing in unison. Listen closely to each other's heartbeats and breaths. Stay in the hug until you are both completely relaxed, with no expectations of sex, though if you progress to sex, that is fine.

Another nice addition to the shrink wrap hug is the twenty-second hug and six-second kiss. Kiss for a minimum of six seconds and do not count out loud, just linger! Don't pressure each other to expect sex. Research reports that hugging for twenty seconds or longer releases oxytocin, a "love chemical" in the body. Simply enjoy the pleasure and closeness of kissing and hugging. These easy techniques can decrease anxiety and help you warm up to each other until your erotic energy is flowing naturally again. Focus on pleasure and relaxation, not creating desire, and make sure you go in for those six-second kisses and twenty-second hugs as often as you can!

8. **Steam it up**

Heat, steam, and sweat equals hot bodies, loose muscles, low stress, and a resurgence of desire. Heat can be a great aphrodisiac, especially if you let enough sweat build up to create slipping and sliding. Turn up the thermostat and run a hot shower to create your own at-home steam room. Meet each other in the shower with your favorite soaps, oils, lotions, or toy, with lights on or off. Can you imagine the fun you might have groping in the steam being unable to see? How about a vertical shrink wrap hug in the shower? Another way to create sexual heat is to seal yourselves under a pile of covers. Use several down comforters to guarantee that the sweat will pour, and don't forget the "No kids, no pets, no disturbances sign!"

9. Open Your Eyes

Open your eyes to each other in a new way, literally! Get face to face in a shrink wrap hug, focus on each other, and keep your eyes open for the entire experience. This is a powerful way to create an intense sexual and emotional experience and let your partner know that you are completely in tune and connected in that moment. Eyes on your partner only, and don't blink for the best part, the intense ending of climax.

10. The case for dirty little secrets

The use of fantasies to fuel your sex drive is a normal and healthy part of human sexuality, and it can jumpstart your desire even more if you share with your partner. But first have a conversation about whether or not you are both open to hearing each other's secret thoughts. If either of you feel it's too uncomfortable or emotionally risky, then you may want to keep your fantasies to yourself. However, I encourage you to try to open in this way. Secondly, reassure each other about your faithfulness, boundaries, and keeping your commitment to not act out with emotional or physical affairs. Sharing private fantasies can also help to affair-proof your relationship. If you've never shared with your partner, go ahead, 'fess up! If you can be open with your private thoughts, you can provide your partner with very useful information about what you find attractive and turns you on.

Sharing your fantasies and crushes doesn't mean you will act on them. In fact, the reverse is true. Most people never actually act on fantasies. They are simply thoughts that can be a sexual energizer to bring you closer and minimize the risk of affairs. The threat of attraction to another person can keep your partner awake to the fact that you are still attracted, attractive, and sexually alive. In research on the brain in love by Dr. Helen Fisher, Rutgers University anthropologist, jealousy and possessiveness are actually healthy, normal human characteristics. Simply because you are in a committed relationship doesn't mean your fantasies and attractions to others are dead. It is also normal human nature to be "scanning the environment" for potential mates, even if you are in a happy long-term relationship. That doesn't mean you are planning to seek out infidelity, it just means you are alive and still have the need for the excitement of erotic in your life.

11. Get back to your future

The sexuality of your younger years is still within your memory and may hold important clues about how to rejuvenate your intimacy. It may need to be adapted because you've changed physically, but your skill set remains. Your teenage and young adult years may hold the keys to reinvigorate your sex life in the present and future. Can you remember how you first discovered each other sexually and learned each other's interests, likes, and needs? Did you let your inhibitions go wild, sneak around, or have sex in interesting places? You may have talked about sex openly and directed each other exactly what to do. If you're having trouble getting your erotic energy back or creating new ideas, time travel to your past and think about what you were doing that worked well when you first met.

12. **Bungle, fumble, punt!**

Bungled sex is a comedy of errors, not a tragedy! Let yourself laugh and play with it! When is the last time you had a moment of sex gone wrong? Many couples are *way* too serious about sex, and truth be told, bumbling sex happens to everyone sometime, and it can be hysterically funny. A certain amount of "sexual bloopers" are a given at any age. You must admit, when you really think about the mechanical details of sex, it's a wonder it ever actually works at all! It's very common to fumble sex in the beginning before a couple gets in sync and really knows each other's bodies, likes, and dislikes. It's also common to bungle it as you age because your interests, physical ability, and endurance may change.

Aging is not a death knell for sexuality, but you may need to change your expectations of great sex. There is much more to it than hours of intercourse. You may opt for just foreplay, shrink wrap hugs, kissing and hugging, climaxing in different ways, or just falling asleep in each other's arms. If it's one of those times when it's just not going well, there's nothing wrong with saying, "Okay, maybe not!" Make sure you allow yourselves to simply enjoy the ridiculousness of a sexual fumble and laugh! There's always next time!

Sparkling Point

Sex is about "being with" more so than the "doing to" that sustains lovers over time. The way you connect to each other in your humanness and vulnerability as you age provides the emotional glue that can keep your sex life vibrant for the long haul.

Remember that the erotic is a much bigger concept than just sex. It's any experience that awakens your passion for living, joy, adventure, discovery, and purpose. No matter how long you've been together or how much you've changed, if you've let your erotic energy fade, it is still possible to re-create it, or create it for the first time. If you're a young or new couple, enjoy every minute and do more of what is working well for you now. If you are in midlife or your senior years, it's not necessary to have high drive and the wild sex you might have had in your younger years. You may need to redefine great sex at this stage of life and adjust your expectations. Project yourself into a successful future and visualize the details of how you can refresh your pleasure and desire. Use the twelve tips in this chapter as a starting point to create or imagine your own unique solutions.

❖ PLAY # 22

The Triple Threat Secret of "Great Couples"

1. On a scale of 1-10, rate your relationship for the following:

   Fun   ____

   Friendship   ____

   Companionship   ____

   In order to restart your fun, friendship, and companionship, consider what simple pleasures are present in your life that you can increase right now to experience more joy and laughter?

   What fun experiences did you have when you first got together that you can start doing again?

   What were your favorite ways to have fun as a child?

   What fun are you saving for your future that you can start doing right now?

2. Begin to reconnect to being great friends by answering the following questions:

   My definition of a great friend is...

   What efforts am I making to be a great friend? What am I giving?

   The ways my partner shows friendship that mean the most to me are...

The best times and places to check in as friends and share support are…

Brainstorm a list of ways you can create more fun, friendship, and companionship. Anything goes, so be outrageous and do not edit yourself!

Create three "sneaky surprises" for your partner that you think will create outrageous fun and increase your feeling of togetherness.

Play # 22

Takeaway Notes

❖ PLAY # 23

The Perfect Day

Imagine and describe the perfect day you both would find fun, adventurous, and exciting. Write a short news story your perfect day with this headline and opening line:

Local Couple Has Perfect Day

One of the GREAT COUPLES, (Your Names)_____

had their perfect day together. They...

1. Review your lists of all possible solutions for potential fun. Choose your top 3 activities: Fun:

   1.

   2.

   3.

   Friendship and Companionship:

   1.

   2.

   3.

   Now choose the one you most want to start doing now:

During the next week, answer the following and text or email your answers to your partner:

I heard that you have the most fun when we......

I understand that you feel I am your best friend when I...

When it comes to keeping our fun, friendship, and companionship vibrant, I promise to give you...

In one week's time, re–rate your fun, friendship, and companionship on a scale of 1 to 10.

Fun   ____

Friendship   ____

Companionship   ____

If your numbers are higher than the first time, discuss what has contributed to the improvement. If your numbers are the same as the first time, discuss what you both can do to raise them one point. If your numbers are lower, discuss what you have forgotten to do or lost track of, and how you can re-energize.

Play # 23

Takeaway Notes

❖ PLAY # 24

Fueling Your Erotic

In terms of affection and sex, what do you want more of:

More:

Less:

Same:

Brainstorm and list 10 ideas you are willing to try to reinvigorate pleasure and desire.

Share your answers to the questions above with your partner. Evaluate yourselves with respect to the ten tips below. Share feelings and ideas about each, and discuss what you each want and don't want.

1. Staging your sanctuary

2. Styling each other

3. Sexy shopping spree

4. Do one thing different

5. Shrink wrap hugs, twenty second hugs, and six second kisses

6. Steam it up

7. Eyes open

8. Sharing fantasies and crushes

9. Techniques from your younger years

10. Ability to laugh about sex

Play # 24

Takeaway Notes

❖ **PLAY # 25**

Fanning The Embers

An excellent way to become comfortable with one another again is to get into bed or sit on the couch together, skin to skin, and simply hold and hug until you feel completely relaxed. You may talk or not – your call, but sure to follow the guideline of no problem talk or discussion of issues during this time. The point is to create bonding, holding, and an emotionally safe time. There must be a clear agreement between you and your partner that there is no expectation holding and hugging progresses to sex. Although if it naturally does, that is fine. You can relax and have pillow talk, or you may wish to share your favorite ways to be cuddled and hugged. Be careful to keep your conversation kind and respectful and make sure you share without criticism or judgement.

A suggestion is, with your hands, show your partner how you like to be held, hugged, and touched. Say "I really like this, that's the best way, that's my favorite way, or my most comfortable way". If there is something you do not care for, simply say: "that way, not as much, not my favorite, or I'm not comfortable that way".

Play # 25

Takeaway Notes

❖ PLAY PRACTICE # 26

Re–Ignite Your Sexual Sparkle

Begin with a reassessment of how you feel about your intimacy yourself and in relation to your partner.

On a scale of 1-10, rate, how satisfied are you with your intimacy/sexuality/affection?

On a scale of 1-10, how much fun, joy, and playfulness is there in your sexual life?

What sparkling moments are you creating for yourself?

What sparkling moments are you and your partner creating together that you want to continue or increase?

If a miracle happened, what would be happening in your intimate life? Be specific about what you and your partner would be doing?

Is there anything about your own sexuality, wishes, needs, desires, or fantasies that you have not shared with your partner?

Eroticism is anything that brings you the thrill of living, List experiences or actions that you feel would bring more eroticism into your relationship.

What stands in the way of sharing these intimate thoughts, wishes, and desires with your partner?

Do you have any fears about your partner's reaction?

What would you need in order to feel safe sharing with your partner?

What differences would make a difference to your partner?

Where are you both willing to begin?

What is the easiest and most do-able step?

What are your boundaries?

What are you willing to try that may be new or different?

Play # 26

Takeaway Notes

❖ PLAY PRACTICE # 27

Reno and Re -Styling

A sanctuary is a place of refuge and safety. Think of your bedroom as your sexual private bubble for rejuvenation and refreshment. It is a wonderful place to block out worries, concerns, and simply relax, refresh, enjoy, and play. Look at your bedroom and ask: is this a place I would find appealing for a date? Is it a pleasing place to recharge, get close, and enjoy one another's company? Your bedroom should be comfortable, enticing, and stimulating to all the senses. List all possible ideas about how you would like to renovate your sexual sanctuary: your bedroom. Share and discuss your ideas with each other.

Another area of pleasure to consider is re-styling yourselves. The goal is to tune into your partner's sensual, erotic side, and once you know the details of what each of you like, please each other by providing those experiences. Discuss your style together, and list what you desire, and the actions you will both take.

Play # 27

Takeaway Notes

❖ PLAY # 28

Do One Thing Different

Love is a verb. You have to act, not just wish or hope. It takes consistent action by partners to keep their intimate life vibrant and growing. Important that both partners initiate sex, because if that falls on one person, it often leads to feelings of resentment, rejection, and low self-esteem.

Make a list of different sexual activities you would like to try. Discuss with your partner. Decide which are your top three, which is your number one, and which is the most do-able place to begin.

Play # 28

Takeaway Notes

❖ PLAY # 29

Welcome to Fantasyland

Sharing fantasies about your crushes, whether they be celebrities or real people in your life, can provide great information for your partner, such as what kind of look is most attractive to you and what turns you on. Be sure to agree on what is acceptable to share and what your partner may find threatening or hurtful. Also be clear about your commitment to not to act on your fantasies.

Share:

What did you like best about each other's fantasies?

Play # 29

Takeaway Notes

❖ PLAY # 30

Bring on the Heat!

Heat is a great aphrodisiac, so turn it up and add an extra layer of sensuality to your intimate life and create a great motivator for foreplay. There are infinite number of ways to turn on the heat. Make a list of ten ideas for foreplay that may add some heat to your sex life. Be creative, don't edit yourselves, and make sure you discuss likes, dislikes, and boundaries.

Play # 30

Takeaway Notes

Sparkling Points Summary

Despite the challenges of long - term relationships and aging, you shouldn't settle for a life without affection and passionate sex. Doing so can harm your physical, emotional, intellectual, and spiritual well-being, and put you at risk for outside temptations to fill that void. There is another option: re - ignite your erotic energy! If you don't keep fueling your erotic energy, the fire will eventually burn out.

It is a mistake to try to reignite your sexual intimacy without first reinvigorating the other areas of your relationship first: emotional connection, friendship, companionship and fun.

The triple - threat secret GREAT couples know: fun, friendship, and companionship fuel passion!

There is a simple solution to reignite your erotic energy: restart your joy, fun. friendship, and companionship first!

No matter how long you've been disconnected, if you started out as great friends, you can re-create that togetherness.

Create a sanctuary for intimacy by making your bedroom sensually enticing and comfortable.

Do one thing different. Try a new move each time you make love.

Shrink wrap hugs, six second hugs, and six second kisses are a good way to start warming up the embers of erotic passion.

Sharing private fantasies and secret crushes can turn up your sexual heat and affair-proof your relationship.

Your younger years hold clues to reawakening your sex life in the present and future.

Remember: sex is "FOR PLAY!"

Over the long haul, erotic love can be sustained when sex is about "being with" more so than "doing to". The way you connect to each other in your humanness and vulnerability as you age provides the emotional glue that can keep your sex life vibrant for a lifetime.

PART 3

Still Stuck

CHAPTER 7

Breaking the Bad

Words of Wisdom

Tell me how you were loved and I'll tell you how you love.

- Esther Perel, author of *Mating in Captivity*

How do you break the chain of trauma and illness whose price is compounded with each successive generation? At the end of the day, the way we honor our parents and their efforts is by carrying on their blessings and doing our best to not pass forward their troubles, their faults to our own children. It's only through the hard work of transformation so those of ours who have come before cease to be the ghosts that haunt us.

- Bruce Springsteen, from *US* by Terry Real

Family pathology is like a fire in the woods, taking down all in front of it, until someone turns to face the flames

- Terry Real, Psychotherapist and author of <u>US</u>

You are being led around by your wounded child, and your reaction to the trauma you experienced. It's not just that you may have had trauma, it's that you were left alone with it and what you did in reaction to it. 95 per cent of trauma is multi - generational, that's just how it works. We unwittingly pass it on, whatever was passed on to you happened through your parents' experience in life which they hadn't quite resolved by the time they had you.

- Dr. Gabor Mate, Author of *In the Realm of Hungry Ghosts*

Each person is suffering from their own emotional poison, it has nothing to do with you. Your reactions come from beliefs that are deep inside of you. You have been conditioned to be a certain way, and you have repeated your reactions thousands of times. Your challenge is to take a risk and make different choices and change your reactions. You have to change again and again and keep changing until you get what you want.

- Miguel Ruiz, author of Mastery of Love

Why are you still stuck?

If you find after doing the work of searching for sparkle, going for gold, and igniting your erotic, there is still little to no improvement in your relationship, you are most likely stuck in the dysfunction of generational curses. That may sound serious, but it is not hopeless! Don't give up yet! Most of us marry our "unfinished business". There is hope and infinite possibility that these patterns can change, but it has to begin with you looking in the mirror and acknowledging your truth about your experience with love.

How you were loved is how you love. From the day you were born, you have observed with curious wonder not only how you were being loved, but also how your parents were loving each other. You were also observing how generations before you loved as well. Their legacy has been passed on to you to become the blueprint for your relationships as well as for your children and their children. If you are stuck in destructive patterns, you are being held hostage by the legacy of loving that you inherited. Those patterns settled deeply into your core sense of yourself and determine how you love.

Experts know that humans are attracted to what is experienced in childhood. Unfortunately, we tend to be most attracted to the family member with whom we had the worst relationship. In the early 1900s, Sigmund Freud defined this as "repetition compulsion". He stated that the undeniable power of attraction lies in our unconscious, and we are all repeating or repairing patterns embedded deeply in infancy and childhood. This is what I call "blueprint baggage": your trauma and relationship dysfunctional patterns.

Sparkling Point

Your "blueprint baggage" is the trauma and relational dysfunction that has been passed down through the generations of your family. These emotional ghosts may be ruining your present relationship.

Why the deep dive is important

How can you transform a toxic legacy? The next step in healing will require you to take a deep dive into your family history and its relationship patterns in order to break your generational curses. This is vital in order to both heal and pass along to the younger generations coming up. The "how" is to start learning what you are bringing to your partnership that is not serving you. The next step will be for you and your partner to work together to break out of toxic patterns.

Sparkling Point

You may still be stuck because relationship patterns transmitted through generations of your family are leading you. If left to fester, these patterns transform into "generational curses" that will continue to determine your future unless they are broken.

How we learn to love

As an infant, you were already learning about love by how your family members were treating one another. The intense mind/body connection between mother and baby is well known, and babies sense both well – being and distress in their mother and environment. Even in your first days, you were picking up signals about whether your family was a safe, nurturing place. Babies learn the instant they enter this world if they will be fed when hungry, kept warm when cold, and comforted when lonely and distressed. If there was happiness, peacefulness, and emotional safety in your home, you already had a good foundation for your future.

Sparkling Point

If your basic needs were consistently met and you were loved well in childhood, there is an excellent chance you learned how to love and be loved well.

However, if your world wasn't safe and nurturing, and your family environment was plagued by hostility, emotional coldness, neglect, abuse, or violence, you most likely learned that relationships can be depriving, unsafe, and even dangerous. If you were raised in an environment where mental illness or substance abuse were present, you may have learned that the world was scary and dangerous. Perhaps an explosive, drunk parent could rage through the house, throw dishes, and abuse you and everyone else. You may have witnessed a severely depressed parent who had no energy to deal with you. Or you may have been traumatized by the manic rampages of a parent with bipolar disorder or the psychotic breaks of one with schizophrenia.

Over time these traumatic experiences become deeply embedded into the unconscious mind. As a child grows, patterns of relating observed first-hand have an impact on their ability to be close, experience healthy intimacy, communicate well, manage anger, and resolve conflict. These patterns are imprinted very early into a child's core being and sense of self. They become toxic generational curses until someone has the courage to face themselves and their patterns, and slay their monsters.

The big and small of trauma

There is a faulty belief that trauma occurs from only disastrous, tragic events such as severe abuse, war, violent crimes, or other losses. But trauma can also occur from death by a thousand small cuts that can be just as debilitating as major disastrous events. In his book, *The Mastery of Love*, Miguel Ruiz states there are both overt and covert types of emotional poison in families that create "emotional hell" and leave a legacy of trauma. The trauma begins in the family of origin, and most of us become "the walking wounded", carrying some form of childhood trauma.

Almost everyone that has entered my office for therapy has described some form of trauma. I've heard about families that were cold, unaffectionate, silent, where children felt invisible, without care or comfort. Others described families that were so rigid and controlled that suppression of all emotion was a requirement. I've also heard of severe, chronic neglect from those who were forgotten at school, whose parents never attended their activities, or spoke to them. Then there are the more serious cases of violence, substance abuse, sexual abuse, untreated mental illness, and legacies of secrets that would drive any human into mental illness as an escape.

I once had a client describe how proud he was that he was left home alone at the age of five, and how he had gotten used to being isolated and lonely. He was unaware that in his marriage he was repeating the same childhood experiences by ignoring his wife and son, fending for himself, and spending most of his time alone. The survival skill that enabled him to survive when he was five was ruining his marriage and damaging his relationship with his son.

Another client shared his memories that nothing he did was ever good enough. He was constantly demeaned by both parents, told he was bad, and never complimented even though he was a high achiever. He continued overachieving in adulthood, creating a career in finance and accumulating wealth. For decades his narcissistic parents used him as their private bank, demanding that he provide unlimited money and buy them multiple homes, even as they squandered their own money on shopping and gambling.

Sometimes my clients tell these heartbreaking stories through tears and giggles, all the while pleading: "it was fine, it was fine, I had a wonderful, happy childhood." I know better. It was not fine, and their trauma is alive and well, destroying their relationships one by one. This is where the difficult therapeutic work must begin, gently peeling away the trauma, so a person can grow into a wise, mature adult who can love profoundly.

In an interview with Prince Harry by noted trauma expert and physician Dr. Gabor Mate, I was intrigued by Prince Harry's recollection of his youth. He was well aware that his father had a mistress, that his mother was being emotionally destroyed because of it, and that his parents' marriage was in shambles. Harry recalled the traumatic way he learned of his mother's death, relating that his father, now King Charles, came into his room in the middle of the night, told him his mother was dead, patted him on the knee, and left him alone without as much as a comforting hug.

One can only imagine how a twelve-year-old brain could cope with such trauma. It is no wonder that through his early adulthood, Harry held onto the belief that his mother had simply gone into hiding, and believed that she would return to him when it was safe to do so. It is also not surprising that Harry acted out with substances in his young adult life. The wonderful part of his story is that he has faced his generational curses and has done The therapeutic work to heal his unresolved grief and family dysfunction. No doubt his children and their children will benefit in deep ways from the therapeutic work he has done.

Dr. Mate offers his belief that ninety-five per cent of trauma is not caused by big crises, but evolves from trauma transmitted down through generations of the family. Unhealthy ways of relating remain unresolved in those that came before you, and therefore, you carry the memories of those burdens within you and guide the way you are loving in the present. A wounded child who was left alone with their trauma as Prince Harry was, will continue to be in charge of his adult life, something no child should ever have to do. Allowing the traumatized child version of you to run your life and relationships is a guaranteed disaster waiting to happen.

Missing adult skills

Unfortunately, very few of us enter adult relationships with the skills needed for healthy loving. This arises from the fact that as children we don't have the emotional or cognitive capacity to learn mature, adult relationship skills. Think about the coping capacities you had as a child. They were most likely few and far between, and not very effective. What can children actually do when they are upset, angered, insulted, frightened, or sad? I ask adults what they remember about their coping style as children.

The typical reactions I hear are: impulsive acting out behaviors such as silence, hiding, isolating, fleeing, tantrums, or lies. I also have heard such statements as: "I ran and hid, I held my feelings in and cried silently by myself, I just stayed silent because I was afraid, I fought back and my anger was out of control, or I turned to sex, drugs, and rock and roll."

Your triggers

Childhood adaptation follows us into adult relationships. Ask yourself how your immature, ineffective coping skills show up in your present adult relationship. Problems arise when familiar scenarios show up and your automatic, adaptive childhood behaviors activate. Your brain is highjacked by the memory of those experiences and you react with the only responses you had available to you as a child. For example, if you experienced silent treatment, removal of affection, threats of abandonment, yelling, screaming, berating, or physical violence, in your adult relationship your childhood survival skills will kick in. You may respond in unhealthy ways such as silent treatment, defensiveness, attacking, arguing to win, or even physical violence. If both partners wounds are reopened simultaneously, and neither has done the work to release trauma and learn new skills, the couple will most likely continue to go down the rabbit hole of destructive patterns. That is when you are most likely to do harm to each other and the relationship.

Sparkling Point

Trauma from the past lurks like a thief in the night, ready to pounce and rob your mature, adult brain of its ability to be loving and wise in relationships.

Although emotional triggers are deeply imprinted in your memory, you can quickly change them by shifting your focus to new skills. Once you learn to manage your own reactions, it is important to tune in and discover your partner's hot buttons. You may not be aware of each other's triggers, so it is important to discuss them and listen very closely about behavior that bothers your partner. A good starting point is for each of you to ask the other what one or two things each does that are most upsetting, then commit not to do those things to one another.

Sparkling Point

Triggers are your emotional soft spots, behaviors that you find upsetting, irritating, and intolerable. They originate from childhood trauma that has not been healed.

When you are triggered by these memories, your rational brain becomes highjacked by raw emotion and the out-of-control hurt child takes over.

Banishing curses

When patterns are so entrenched, can they be broken? The answer is yes, and you can learn new skills that are more mature, respectful, and productive. The purpose of doing this work is to examine your trauma, the patterns in your family of origin, and to become consciously aware of your triggers and reactions. Then the task is to practice and master new patterns and skills and allow them to become habits. If both partners commit to this work, you can return home to love and stay there forever. The goal is to bring you into fully respectful fulfilling love.

I recommend if you are aware that you may have severe trauma, you should do this work with a therapist trained in multigenerational family systems, patterns and trauma. You may need a guide to facilitate this work in the protective, nurturing setting of the therapy room. If you become aware of painful experiences of neglect and abuse, mental illness, substance abuse or violence, the help of a trained therapist will be critical.

If you are comfortable doing this work on your own with the plays that follow, the first step is to become consciously aware of your relational history. You can begin by tracing patterns in your extended family, and exploring areas of strengths and dysfunction. The next task is to examine yourself and the generational curses you have carried forward into your present, followed by releasing that trauma from those experiences, reparenting yourself, and learning wise adult behaviors. Then you will need to practice, practice, practice to become a master of your life and allow your wounded child to be healed.

This is a complex process that may help you immediately, or may take some time. It may be emotional and even painful, but it is a critical mission if you are going to break the legacy of your generational curses. Although my belief is that the triggers from trauma never totally vanish, they can be minimized so that you can love from a healthy emotional place.

Sparkling Point

Never allow your traumatized child to lead your adult relationships again. Breaking your generational curses require you to stand firm in your commitment to look in the mirror, change yourself, and let your partner change you.

❖ PLAY # 31

Designing Your New Blueprint

Your task in this play is to discover what your generational curses are, where they originated and how they are showing up in your present relationship. Your goal will be to trace and track a few major themes in your history, ideally back to at least to your grandparents' generation. If you know important information about earlier generations, write that down as well. You may do your play separately or together.

Let's begin by taking a look at the most significant relational patterns and themes in your family. Think of this as your past story as it relates to your present relationship. Focus on the family patterns that resonate for you now and relate to why you are stuck. Be descriptive with words and phrases that would tell your story to someone else hearing it for the first time. Use your own colorful or poetic words, or whatever family mottoes come to mind. Some examples are: cold, warm, loving, nasty, critical, demeaning, silent, screaming, intimidating, or uninterested. Some examples of descriptive phrases are: she ruled the roost with an iron fist, she wore the pants in the family, he was a drunken terrifying tornado, he was Mr. Jekyll and Dr. Hyde, the women control everything, the women are made of steel, the men all have affairs, the men are silent and passive, there was coldness and no one ever hugged. There were many secrets in the family. No one ever talked about anything important. Illnesses and deaths were never mentioned.

Questions for consideration:

Describe how you were loved:

What emotional poison did you experience?

Who did harmful things to you and what were those?

Who didn't stop them?

Who did you see do it to others?

What patterns do you notice around your family map?

What is your family history of relationship curses?

Which behaviors get repeated in your current relationships?

Who did you turn to for comfort when you were hurt or scared?

What patterns and themes are you noticing across the generations?

What were your parents' and grandparents' marriages like?

Were their marriages healthy or dysfunctional? In what ways?

Were they loving, affectionate, cherishing, respectful?

Was there coldness, hostility, silence, fighting, violence?

What roles did each partner play?

Were there control issues?

Was there pursuing and distancing behaviors?

What messages did you get about yourself from these observations?

Examples:

I am not worthy of love.

I am not worthy of being seen or spoken to.

I am invisible.

I have to beg for and chase love.

I am used to having my needs neglected.

I learned to be a doormat.

I learned to be silent and have no voice.

I learned to be intimidating.

I learned that disrespect is acceptable.

I learned to deal with conflict.

I learned to cope through addictions: substances, sex, pornography, or infidelity.

No one comforted me, I comforted myself.

I learned I had to be perfect to get love.

What were your childhood adaptive modes of coping? Here are some examples:

Silence

Crying

Running away and hiding

Suppressing feelings

Tantrums

Fighting back

Screaming

Hitting

Breaking things

Blaming others

Telling lies

Triggers

Considering the information you have so far, what are the top triggers in your current relationship? What are the ways your partner behaves that evoke a negative automatic reaction in you?

Describe your familial generational curses.

What are the issues that you most want to change from your generational curses?

What are the one or two interactions that are your worst triggers?

What are your partner's one or two worst triggers?

What do you want to request that your partner be aware of and commit not to do to you?

What do you want to commit to absolutely watch for and not do to your partner?

Courageous conversation with your partner:

Share the important information you have learned from this play: family patterns, generational curses, how they are affecting you now, and what you most want to address.

Play # 31

Takeaway Notes

❖ PLAY # 32

Your Evolving You: A Visualization

Let's solidify your learning into your unconscious, knowing that the sparkling moments you have gained in the course of reading this book and contemplating your relationship will be there for you as you need to call upon them.

Let's begin:

Get into a relaxed position close to your partner. Choose the most comfortable position to be physically connected to each other, such as cuddling side by side, or holding hands.

Begin to focus on your breathing and relaxing all your muscles.

Slow your breath and breathe deeper and deeper, more slowly each time.

With each breath, imagine taking in pure, life-giving air. With each exhale, imagine blowing the toxins and distress out of and away from your body.

Sync your breathing with each other by taking ten deep breaths together.

Feel each other's heartbeat and listen to each other's breaths as you continue to relax.

Imagine filling your entire body with clear blue sky and warm sunshine.

Repeat:

> I am calm and relaxed,
> I am calm and relaxed,
> I am calm and relaxed.

Start at the top of your head and picture each muscle in your body beginning to loosen and relax.

Focus first on your head, temples and neck.

Next release all the tension in your shoulders and the top of your back.

Picture your stress flowing down your arms and out your fingertips. Continue relaxing your chest, stomach, and abdominal muscles, letting go of stress. Keep letting the stress flow down your legs and out through the bottom of your feet and toes.

Continue breathing deeply and slowly as you continue to let go of all stress and toxins.

Repeat again:

> I am calm and relaxed
> I am calm and relaxed.
> I am calm and relaxed.

Repeat:

> I invite in that which I desire: new love, new growth, and new learning.
> I invite in that which I desire: new love, new growth, and new learning.
> I invite in that which I desire: new love, new growth, and new learning.

As you continue to relax, imagine that a miracle is happening to your relationship right at this moment. The miracle is bringing you joy, passion, contentment, and love.

As this miracle is swirling about you, imagine beginning to walk hand and hand with your partner down a beautiful path. Along the way, smell the refreshing fragrances, and feel the gentle breeze and pleasant warmth of the sun on your skin. See yourselves arriving at the end of the path where you each find your younger selves sitting by a large suitcase.

This version of you may be carrying hurts and disappointments from an earlier time in your life. These may be small hurts that have accumulated over your first eighteen years of life. You may also be carrying the heaviest of loads, the generational curses of your ancestors that have been passed down to you through your parents' experiences, your grandparents' experiences, and generations that came before them. Remember, they too have experienced the challenges you are facing now.

Now there is a beautiful golden pedestal next to the two little versions of you and your partner. Upon it sits a sparkling crystal ball that tells the stories of miracles to come in your future.

Now each take the younger versions of yourself by the hand and hold on tightly. Tell them.

"We are going to go on a journey, and you will be safe and protected. You are going to leave behind the suitcases since they are no longer needed or useful. I am going to take the lead now and guide you, and I will stand before you if you feel frightened. Your job is simply to enjoy life and have fun. You are no longer in charge, nor will you need to be in charge of anything. That's my job now."

With little you in tow, get closer and gaze into the crystal ball; notice that a gentle breeze begins to blow, carrying along winds of change and creative solutions These winds carry with them miracles made of sparkling moments and all possibilities for change for a future of shared joy, compassion, synchronicity, peacefulness, calm, passion, and the eroticism of a thrilling life worth living. These are yours to use as you get unstuck, reclaim the love you deserve, and banish the generational curses of trauma and that are holding you back.

Gaze into the miracle crystal ball for as long as you wish. Allow yourself to see your future joy, your children's future of healthy loving, and their children's future, your grandchildren, and great-grandchildren basking in the joy of healthy loving, and no longer carrying the heavy load of those generational curses.

Fast forward to near the end of your life. See yourself at that moment being happy in your relationship. Take note of having given and received love with your partner through the years and the contentment this has brought. See your happiest moments of joy, passion, affection, and closeness. Appreciate the comfort and love you have given and received in the most difficult times of your life together, the storms you have weathered.

If you have children, them with you at this future point in their life, enjoying successful, happy, loving relationships of their own. See the legacy you have left in the joy and laughter of your children, and their children. Let yourself feel complete fulfillment and contentment, as you observe what your children have learned about loving from you.

Simply sit now, in peace and quiet, for a few moments and bask in the warmth and glow of the love you have created, given, and received. Celebrate the loving partner you have become, the admiration your partner has for you, and what you admire about them.

Focus on your gratitude for the love your partner has given to you, and who he or she has become. Continue breathing deeply and relaxing your entire body.

Take as much time as you wish to hold this picture of the happy, loving outcome you see in your future in your miracle of your love restored.

Rest peacefully in the knowledge that, free from the baggage and curses of the past, you have the solutions, strengths, and capabilities within you to bring about this happy future not only for yourself, but for generations to come.

Once again, the gentle breezes of the winds of change return and begin to blow and guide you back on the path to the present. Begin to walk on that path to journey back to the present moment.

Remember that the little wounded, hurt version of you will always be with you, but no longer needs to be in charge of fighting your battles. You are now in charge and you are already keeping the child within you safe and protected. As you return to the present, take a few moments to see your reclaimed relationship and what you will be doing today, tomorrow, next week, next month, and next year. Imagine taking your first steps right now and, in the next few moments, allow as much time as you need to re-orient yourself to the present. Whenever you are ready, in your own time, come back to the room and open your eyes.

As you return, keep this thought deeply within you: Your love is a precious gift, so take each and every day as an opportunity to make it a whole season of love.

Play # 32

Takeaway Notes

CHAPTER 7

Sparkling Points Summary

Your "blueprint baggage" is the trauma and relational dysfunction that has been passed down through the generations of your family. These emotional ghosts are ruining your present relationship.

You may still be stuck because patterns transmitted down through generations are leading you. If left to fester, these patterns transform into "generational curses" that will continue to determine your future generations to come. If your basic needs were consistently met in childhood, there is an excellent chance you learned how to love and be loved well.

Trauma from the past lurks, ready to pounce and rob your mature, adult brain of your ability to be loving and wise in your relationships. Triggers are emotional soft spots, behaviors that you find upsetting, irritating, and intolerable. They originate from your unique childhood experiences and unhealed trauma.

When you are triggered by the memory of your childhood trauma, never again allow your traumatized child to lead your adult relationships. Breaking your generational curses also require you to stand firm in your commitment to look in the mirror and change yourself, and let your partner change you.

CHAPTER 8

Easy to Love

Words of Wisdom

If one advances confidently in the direction of his dreams, and endeavors to live the life which he has imagined, he will meet with a success unexpected in common hours. He will put some things behind, will pass an invisible boundary; new, universal, and more liberal laws will begin to establish themselves around and within him.

- Henry David Thoreau, poet

You are what you do, not what you say you will do.

- Carl Jung, psychiatrist

Do or do not, there is no try.

- Yoda, *Star Wars* character

Everything is made of love; love is life itself. We can create a life with love, a masterpiece of art. To become masters of love we must practice love. Love is action.

- Miguel Ruiz, Author, *Mastery of Love*

Love is The Answer

Falling in love is just the beginning of the magnificent adventure of loving for a lifetime. To be chosen and desired by a soulmate is one of life's most treasured gifts, the miracle cure that heals essential loneliness. Being securely attached to another gives meaning to life, and is what we humans long for the most. And yet, if not nurtured and protected, love can easily deteriorate and die. You are the guardians of the flame of your love, and whether your love lives or dies is now in your hands.

Sparkling Point

Life's greatest prize is an appropriate mating partner. Romantic love is a drive, and addiction, perfectly wonderful when it is going well, horrible when it is going poorly.

- Dr. Helen Fisher, anthropologist

The challenge ahead

Loving well and staying in love is never a done deal. Now that you have read *The Return to Love Playbook* and practiced the plays, you have the seeds of solutions and skills to move forward into a more fulfilling relationship that lasts. The challenge before you now is to stay committed to taking consistent action every single day. This requires mutual give and take, providing emotional holding and safety, and the ability to be selfless. You must continue to risk opening completely and learning from one another. It also involves continuing to work on changing yourself and letting your partner change you. Everlasting love is something you DO, taking action every day to insure your connection stays strong and continues to grow.

Sparkling Point

True intimacy is the continuous joining of two people in deep love and commitment. It is the antidote for the loneliness and despair of the human condition and requires risking the continual opening of yourself to another by sharing the deepest emotional, intellectual, physical, spiritual, and sexual parts of yourself.

To stay or go: one last check

Even though you have done the work in *The Return to Love Playbook*, you may still be struggling with your decision. Several outcomes exist: doing well and staying together, doing well but remaining worried, confused, or unclear about separating. Even if you are sure you are doing well; I expect you to have some doubt about whether your improvement is only a temporary fix. Also, despite heroic efforts, some of you may not make it. It's extremely disheartening to me when a couple does the hard work to stay together but the relationship is too far gone. It also deeply saddens me when I see couples who were once madly in love, had a great foundation, and are decent people, but choose to give up before doing the work to repair their relationship. Prior to making your final decision, you owe it to yourself to run one last check and weigh the risks and benefits of staying versus leaving.

The decision to leave a relationship is rarely easy, and it's an extremely personal decision with many complexities. Before you make up your mind, trust your gut, intuition, and the signals your body may be giving you. If you're experiencing chronic depression, anxiety, or frequently becoming physically ill, your unhappy relationship may be the root cause. If you've made a sincere effort, and either or both of you are still feeling emotionally or physically harmed, then I do not recommend that you stay together. Life is short, and I don't believe people should suffer or remain in relationships that are toxic, neglectful, or abusive. If this is the case, I challenge you to consider why you are choosing to stay in a relationship that is clearly harming your well-being. I recommend you pursue your own individual therapy to examine how you got stuck, why you made your choices, and what trauma may have contributed to them.

I also recommend that you stay committed to practicing the solutions and skills you developed in the *Return to Love Playbook* for at least three to six months. If the techniques do not work for you on your own, find a qualified couples' therapist and give therapy a three-to-six- month trial. After that length of time, if you can honestly say there is no improvement, it may indeed be time for you to consider whether continuing in the current relationship is right for you.

I encourage you to return to your original assessment and review your answers to those questions. Rate yourselves again and take a look at how your ratings have changed.

Consider what you need to keep doing more of to raise your numbers. Here are a few final questions to help you reassess your decision-making:

Is my relationship making my life better or worse? Is it more helpful or harmful to my well-being?

On a scale of 1-10, how happy am I? Is that number acceptable to me?

On a scale of 1-10, how much am I suffering emotionally, physically, spiritually, or sexually?

Have I truly given my all to return to love?

If I walk away, can I do so with no regrets and a clear conscience that I have Given it my best effort?

Is there another secret to making love last?

You might be wondering if I have one last secret for you about how to make love last. While I believe miracle cures can show up, and holding onto hope is critical as well, here's the real secret:

Sparkling Point

The secret to fulfilling, everlasting love is: YOU!

You have had the secret to loving inside you all along! You are the master of your capacity to love! You will be fulfilled if you commit to relentless action to make love last.

If you had good enough parenting and family life in childhood, you have lived the experience of healthy love. Hopefully, you have had the experience of sparkle, the sense of erotic joy and adventure of living. I also hope you have had the good fortune to live in a family where the gold standards of love were practiced by the role models of your parents and older generations. I also hope you observed a positive attitude about affection, passion, and sexuality.

In addition to what you already know and have brought into your relationship, I hope that through the process of doing the plays in *The Return to Love Playbook* you are becoming experts at searching for and creating sparkle, creating gold standards, igniting your erotic passion, and breaking generational curses. My hope is that you are making "the big shift" away from problems, destructive interactions, and harmful generational patterns.

Sparkling Point

Love is a force of nature and the spirit within you that can grow by your innate capacity to love.

This is your birthright and your natural instinct can bring you forward even if you have not experienced healthy love before. If your childhood was troubled, I hope the knowledge and skills in this book have convinced you that you can learn how to love. Remember, failure and practice are the mother of skill and mastery, and that certainly applies to love. Failure is also an opportunity to improve your strategy. You can still learn to create a better love and bring it into your future. Now it's time for you to move forward and trust that every problem in your relationship has infinite solutions, and you and are the best architects to design those solutions.

Sparkling Point

YOU are the secret to keeping your love alive! Childhood experiences of the sparkle and gold of loving are deep inside you waiting to return to your consciousness and live again in your present and future!

The natural laws of loving

I offer you a final gift: *ten natural laws of loving*. I encourage you to look around and observe the natural laws of the universe that act as guideposts for fully loving. Consider nature: flora and fauna and the animal kingdom – and its resilience. While nothing lasts forever, and the human journey on this earth is very short, love and connection are our natural birthright. So, start now following the natural laws of loving and begin creating magnificent love, not only with your partner, but also with all those you come into contact with. Remember it costs nothing to give love away.

Here are the natural laws of loving:

> Love that is meant for you will find you, so intend on it and let go.
> You deserve magnificent, fulfilling love, and anything less is unacceptable.
> The purpose of love is to add to your life, not cause harm and suffering.
> You can stay in love if you intend and follow through with consistent action.
> Life is very short, so NOW is the time for your best effort.
> No relationship is problem-free.
> Differences and conflict are a healthy, necessary part of all relationships
> No one gets everything in a relationship, but you can get much of what you want.
> Your children deserve to be taught how to love well.
> It's easy to love if you practice sparkling moments and gold standards.

When this book found you, you may have felt hopeless and in a great deal of emotional pain. I appreciate the courage it took for you to open *The Return to Love Playbook* and actually, do the work. I celebrate you for your determination not to be part of another broken relationship and divorce. You have much to be proud of because you have made the commitment to create a happier, healthier life for yourself and your loved ones. Most importantly, you are creating a legacy of love for your future generations. If you don't have children; by living in healthy love, you are sending more love out into the world and making it a better place.

Now it is time for you to run on fire towards the most sparkling, fulfilling, resilient, secure, romantic, sexiest love you can imagine and create! I challenge you to continue on your journey, not with fear and pessimism, but with hope, trust, and boldness! Focus on becoming the best individual and lead by example and be the partner you wish to have.

Sparkling Point

Love is your sacred birthright. Claim it and grab the love that you deserve!

Always remember, it's so easy to love!

Love *is* a precious gift, so make each and every day a whole *season* of love!

My love to you always,

Dr. Deb

❖ PLAY # 33

The Way Forward

Take a few moments to consider the commitment you are willing to make to advance your relationship now. Write down the #1 action you are willing to commit to every single day to keep your relationship vibrant.

I commit to…

Share your final promise of commitment with your partner.

Acknowledge and thank your partner for this act of faith.

Play # 33

Takeaway Notes

❖ PLAY # 34

Back to Your Future: A Visualization

Get into a relaxed position close to your partner. Choose the most comfortable position to be physically connected to each other, such as cuddling side by side, in each other's arms, or holding hands. Once you are both comfortable, begin to focus on your breathing and relaxing all your muscles. Slow your breath and breathe deeper and deeper, slower each time. With each breath, imagine taking in pure, life-giving air and with each exhale, imagine blowing the toxins and distress out of and away from your body.

Sync your breathing with each other by taking ten deep breaths together.

Feel each other's heartbeat and listen to each other's breaths as you continue to relax.

Imagine filling your entire body with clear blue sky and warm sunshine.

Say three times: I am calm and relaxed, I am calm and relaxed, I am calm and relaxed.

Start at the top of your head and picture each muscle in your body beginning to loosen and relax.

Focus first on your head, temples and neck.

Next release all the tension in your shoulders and the top of your back.

Picture all your stress flowing down your arms and out your fingertips.

Continue relaxing your chest, stomach, and abdominal muscles, letting go of stress.

Keep letting the stress flow down your legs and out through the bottom of your feet and toes.

Continue breathing deeply and slowly as you continue to let go of all stress and toxins.

Repeat again three times: I am calm and relaxed, I am calm and relaxed, I am calm and relaxed.

As you continue to relax, imagine that a miracle is happening to your relationship right at this moment. It is a miracle that is bringing you into joy, passion, contentment, and love.

As this miracle is swirling about you, imagine beginning to walk hand and hand with your partner down a beautiful path. Along the way, smell the refreshing fragrances, feel the gentle breeze and the pleasant warmth of the sun on your skin. See yourselves arriving at the end of the path where you find an elegantly sculptured pedestal holding a beautiful book crafted of gold. Etched on the cover is the title: *Your Book of Time.*

This is *Your Book of Time*: its pages hold the story of your life from beginning to end. Imagine now that a gentle breeze begins to blow the pages, bringing the winds of change and bringing you to peace, calm, and future happiness. The pages are moving back and forth, back and forth, through all the years of your life.

Now let the pages blow to a moment in your future, near the end of your life. Imagine seeing yourself at that moment in time being the happiest you have ever been in your relationship.

See yourself giving the love you have given to your partner through the years.

See your happiest moments of joy, passion, affection, and closeness.

See the comfort and love you have given and received in the most difficult times of your life together.

If you have children, see them with you at this future point in their life, enjoying successful, happy, loving relationships of their own. See the legacy you have left in the joy and happiness and laughter of your children, and their children.

Let yourself fully feel contentment, as you observe what your children have learned about loving from you.

Simply sit now, in peace and quiet, for a few moments and bask in the warmth and glow of the love you have created, given, and received.

Celebrate the loving, giving partner you have become and the admiration your partner has for you.

Focus on the gratitude you have now for the love your partner has given to you, and who she/he has become.

Continue breathing deeply and relaxing your entire body.

Take as much time as you hold this picture of the happy, loving outcome you now see in your future, in *Your Book of Time.*

Rest peacefully in the knowledge that right NOW you have the solutions, strengths, and capabilities within you to bring about this happy future not only for yourself in your present, but also for the generations of your family to come.

Once again, the gentle breezes of the winds of change return and begin to blow the pages of *Your Book of Time* back to the present.

See what you will be doing today, tomorrow, and next week to begin moving on your journey to reboot your relationship.

Imagine taking your first steps right now.

In the next few moments, take as much time as you need to re-orient yourself to the present.

As you return prepare to return to the room, keep this thought deeply within you:

Your love is a precious gift, so take each and every day as an opportunity and make it a whole season of love.

Whenever you are ready, in your own time, come back to the room and open your eyes.

Play # 34

Takeaway Notes

CHAPTER 8

Sparkling Points Summary

True intimacy is the continuous joining of two people in deep love and commitment. It is the antidote for the loneliness and despair of the human condition and it requires risking the continual opening of yourself to another by sharing the deepest emotional, intellectual, physical, spiritual, and sexual parts of yourself.

The secret to fulfilling love is: YOU! You have had the secret to loving inside you all along! You are the master of your capacity to love!

YOU are the secret to keeping your love alive! Childhood experiences of the sparkle and gold of loving are deep inside you waiting to be called back into your consciousness and lived again in your present and future!

Love is your sacred birthright. Claim it and grab onto the love that you deserve!

And always remember, it's so easy to love!

Love is a force of nature and spirit within you that can grow by opening to your innate capacity to do so.

EPILOGUE

Even though I will always be a member of the broken hearts club, I am now a proud member, and I cherish the club's blessings and gifts. Years ago, my heart was cracked wide open to allow the giving and receiving of more love, passion, and compassion than I ever imagined possible. I have come to understand that grieving lost love and learning to thrive without it was necessary for me to appreciate that love is never guaranteed. Should it find you, nurturing it is a sacred responsibility. When two souls merge, if love is cherished, and there is a relentless commitment to action, it can be magnificent and remain that way for a lifetime.

Reflecting on my journey, the grief of lost love caused me to spiral into a dark period, However, I couldn't see the big picture at the time. I now realize each person who showed up to accompany me out of that dark night had a purpose in furthering my growth. Some have been romantic partners, while others were friends, teachers, and colleagues. Some have become lifelong friends, while others have gone on their way, their mission complete. Each one became a chapter in my love story, and I treasure them all.

My love story isn't over, and I trust it never will be, as it isn't for any of us. As much as I would like to tell you that love has come for me, it hasn't. Still while my heart yearns for love, I am no longer searching for it. Now my perspective comes from a spiritual belief in trusting that if I am meant to merge with another soul in this lifetime, it will happen. Some part of me understands that I wasn't ready before now. I had to grow significantly to become the potential partner I am now with all the relationship skills I have developed. For now, I pour my loving energy into the other aspects of love in relationship with my spirituality, family, friends, colleagues, and clients.

Since I am living it at the moment, I want to reassure you that single life is also a sacred gift to be treasured. If you and your partner have decided to go your separate ways, or you are already single; it is an opportunity to grab life and leap forward to develop yourself and discover that there are other types of love available to you other than romantic love. You can develop more love of self, friends, family, vocation, and avocations. Single life isn't better or worse than life in a relationship, it is simply different. Single life has enabled me to devote myself to my purpose: helping others to learn to love well and stay in love forever.

My journey has brought me to a deep understanding that magnificent love with a cherished partner remains as one of life's most treasured gifts. I also stand firm in my belief that partners CAN return to love and stay there for a lifetime. If you have chosen to do so, you should join together as allies, go to war and fight like hell to resolve your issues! You can create a second relationship with each other that is even better than the first. Your job as a loving partner is never done, because love doesn't survive if left unattended. You must MAKE love happen, that is, take action every single day with relentless commitment.

Whether you decide to return to love, separate, or remain single, the path you are on is meant for you and should be traveled in the service of your personal growth and the higher good. No matter what your relationship status is right now, grab your life and lean into it. Remember, I am on the same journey, striving to become a better person each day, still hoping and dreaming, still making mistakes, and loving it all. My journey through falling in love, young marriage, divorce, dating and lovesickness at midlife, breaking up, and single life has changed me for the good. My broken heart was the beginning of a transformation that brought me home to love and home to myself. And remember, wherever *your* love story takes you, you are already home to love.

Home

Those private moments of anguish, no one knew I feared

Sadness dripped slowly, escaping drudgery inside

Absent contentment forgot the feel of love

A heart once broken,

Now broken open to more: more love, passion, compassion

Connected to source, ascending

Home to love, home to myself, I seek no more

- Dr. Deb

RECOMMENDED READING

Ahrons, C. (1994). *The good divorce: Keeping your family together when your marriage comes apart.* New York: Harper Collins Publishers.

Ban Breathnach, S. (1998). *Something more: Excavating your authentic self.* New York: Warner Books.

Benjamin, J. (1988). *The bonds of love: Psychoanalysis, feminism, and the problem of domination.* New York: Pantheon Books.

Berg, I.K., & Y. Dolan. (1996). *Tales of solutions: A collection of hope inspiring stories.* New York: W.W. Norton and Company.

Brandon, N. (1994). *The six pillars of self esteem.* New York: Bantam Books.

Carlson, R. (1997). *Don't sweat the small stuff.* New York: Hyperion.

Castaldo, D. (2008). *Divorced without children: Solution focused therapy with women at midlife.* New York: Routledge/Taylor & Francis Group.'

Castaldo, D. (2010). *Gifts of love.* Plainfield: Xlibris Press.

Castaldo, D. (2014). *Relationship reboot: Tech support for love.* Denver: Outskirts Press.

Chopra, D. (1994). *The seven spiritual laws of success.* San Rafael: Amber Allen Publishing.

Denniston, P. (2021). *Healing through yoga: Transform your loss into empowerment.* San Francisco: Chronicle Prism.

deShazer, S. (1985). *Keys to solutions in brief therapy.* New York: W. W. Norton and Company.

Fisher, H. (1992). *The Anatomy of Love. The natural history of monogamy, adultery, and divorce.* New York: W.W. Norton and Company.

Fisher, H. (2004). *Why We Love. The nature and chemistry of romantic love.* New York: Holt, Henry and Company.

Fisher, H. (2009). *Why him? Why her? Finding real love by understanding your Personality type.* New York: Holt, Henry, and Company.

Gottman, J.M. (1999). *The seven principles for making marriage work.* New York: Three Rivers Press.

Hanh, T.N. (1991). *Peace is every step.* New York: Bantam Books.

Hanh, T.N. (1998). *Teachings on love.* Berkeley: Parallax Press.

Hanh, T.N. (2001). *Anger.* New York: The Berkley Publishing Group.

Hay, L. L. (1990). *Love yourself, heal your life workbook.* Carson: Hay House, Inc.

Herz Brown, F. (1991). *Reweaving the family tapestry.* New York: W.W. Norton and Company.

His Holiness the Dalai Lama and Cutler, H. (1998). *The art of happiness.* New York: Riverhead Books.

Johnson, S. M. (2008). *Hold me tight: Conversations for a lifetime of love.* New York:

Little, Brown, and Company.

Lerner, H. G. (1985). *The dance of anger.* New York: Harper and Row.

Lerner, H.G. (2009). *The dance of intimacy.* New York: HarperCollins Publishers.

Long, N. and R. Forehand (2002). *Making divorce easier on your child: 50 ways to help children adjust.* New York: Contemporary Books.

Love, P. and S. Stosny (2007). *How to improve your marriage without talking about it.* New York: Crown Publishing Group.

Mate, G. (2022). *The myth of normal: Trauma, illness, and healing in a toxic culture.* New York: Penguin Random House.

McCarthy, B., and E McCarthy (2003). *Rekindling desire: A step by step —by-step program to help low-sex and no-sex marriages.* New York: Taylor & Francis.

Mellody, P. (2003). *Facing Love Addiction: Giving yourself the power to change the way you love.* New York: HarperCollins Publishers.

Nagoski, E. (2021). *Come as you are: The surprising new science that will transform Your sex life.* New York: Simon & Schuster.

Nagoski, E. (2024). *Come Together: The science and art of creating lasting sexual Connections.* New York: Ballantine Books. O'Hanlon, W.H. (2000). *Do one thing different: Ten simple ways to change your life.*

New York: HarperCollins.

Perel, E. (2006). *Mating in captivity: Unlocking erotic intelligence.* New York: HarperCollins Books.

Perel, E. (2017). *The State of Affairs: Rethinking infidelity.* New York: HarperCollins Books.

Real, T. (*1997*). *I don't want to talk about it.* New York: Scribner.

Real, T. (2002). *How can I get through to you.* New York, Simon and Schuster.

Real, T. (2007). *The New Rules of Marriage: What you need to know to make love work.* New York: Ballantine Books.

Real, T. (2022). *Us: Getting past you & me to build a more loving relationship.* New York: Rodale Books.

Ruiz, D. M. (1999). *The Mastery of Love.* San Rafael: Amber-Allen Publishing, Inc.

Schnarch, D. (2003) *The secrets of a passionate marriage: How to increase pleasure and emotional fulfillment in committed relationships.* Victoria: Scribe Publications

Sheehy, G. (1995). *New passages.* New York: Random House.

Spring, J.A. (1997). *After the affair: Healing the pain and rebuilding trust when a partner has been unfaithful.* New York: HarperCollins Publishers.

Wallerstein, J. S. and S. Blakeslee. (1989). *Second chances.* New York: Ticknor and Fields.

Weiner-Davis, M. (1992). *Divorce busting: A revolutionary and rapid program for staying together.* New York: Simon and Schuster.

Printed in the United States
by Baker & Taylor Publisher Services